BAZAAR AND RUMMAGE, GROPING FOR WORDS & WON

This three play volume exhibits to the full Sue Townsend's tal[ ] hilarious comedy from the most painful social insights. 'She is that oddest of theatrical hybrids — a female trickster' *John Lahr*

Bazaar and Rummage brings together a neurotic do-gooder, a tr[ ] [ ]er and three agoraphobics who have been persuaded to ventur[ ] n a jumble sale.
'Ms Townsend has drawn real women, not st[ ]
sharply-observed humour.' [ ] *ress*

'The play is distinguished by sensitive characte[ ]
and affectionate, sometimes sparkling repartee. [ ] ..., *City Limits*

'A very funny play.' Irving Wardle, *Times*

Groping for Words is set in an adult literacy class, where the students' fear of admitting ignorance is as much of a handicap as their inability to read.
'Townsend examines this terror of social judgement as a means of keeping the working class in its place . . . a powerful play.' *New Society*

Womberang shows free spirit Rita Onions bringing joy and anarchy to the grim waiting-room of a gynaecology clinic. 'A daydream of mastered fear.' *New Society*

BAZAAR AND RUMMAGE

GROPING FOR WORDS

&

WOMBERANG

by

SUE TOWNSEND

A Methuen New Theatrescript
Methuen . London and New York

A METHUEN PAPERBACK

First published as a Methuen Paperback original in 1984 by Methuen London Ltd.,
11 New Fetter Lane, london EC4P 4EE and Methuen Inc, 733 Third Avenue,
New York, NY 10017, USA

Set in IBM 10 point Press Roman by 𝄢 Tek-Art, Croydon, Surrey
Printed in Great Britain

British Library Cataloguing in Publication Data

Townsend, Sue
    Bazaar and rummage; Groping for words;
    & Womberang. — (A Methuen new theatrescript)
    I. Title
    822'.914   PR6070.089/

ISBN 0-413-54190-8

CAUTION
All rights in these plays are strictly reserved and application for performance etc.,
should be made to Anthony Sheil Associates Ltd., 2/3 Morwell Street, London
WC1 3AR. No performance may be given unless a licence has been obtained.

Printed in Great Britain by Richard Clay (The Chaucer Press) Ltd, Bungay, Suffolk

BAZAAR AND RUMMAGE

Bazaar and Rummage was first presented in the Royal Court Theatre Upstairs on 10 May 1982, with the following cast:

MARGARET, *a working-class vulgarian, agoraphobic for fifteen years*	Polly Hemingway
BELL-BELL, *an obsessionally clean agoraphobic, who plays the piano*	Liz Kean
FLISS, *a youngish trainee social worker*	Carol Leader
GWENDA, *a middle-aged volunteer social worker, an ex-agoraphobic*	Janette Legge
KATRINA, *an agoraphobic, ex-variety 'songstress'*	Lou Wakefield
WPC, *a woman who is terrified of community policing*	Janette Legge

Directed by Carole Hayman
Music by Liz Kean
Decor by Amanda Fisk
Lighting by Val Claus
Sound by Patrick Bridgeman

ACT ONE

*A multi-purpose church hall in Acton. A
pair of double doors are flanked by two
stained-glass windows. Missing panes of
glass have been replaced by pieces of
coloured cellophane. A garish crucifix
hangs over the doors. Trestle tables and
folding chairs are stacked against a wall.
A piano and a small table complete the
furnishings. An internal door leads to the
lavatory and kitchen.*
    GWENDA and FLISS *enter, GWENDA
is wearing a Crimplene two-piece with a
nylon roll-neck sweater underneath.*
FLISS *is wearing ragged dungarees
(though her boots and shoulder bag are
expensive-looking). They are both
carrying a cardboard box under one arm
and a black plastic bag under the other.*
GWENDA*'s box slides and falls, books
fall out and scatter on the floor.*

GWENDA (*with a small scream*): I said
we were overloaded!

She stands in confusion.

FLISS: No problem.

GWENDA: Here take this. (*She hands
the plastic bag to* FLISS *who is now
overloaded*.)

FLISS (*calmly*): Gwenda, take the bag
from me and put it on the floor.

GWENDA (*scrabbling on the floor
picking up books*): Have you read
Dr Zhivago? (*She holds a book up*.)
I started it but Russian names are so
confusing. I tried calling them Smith
and Jones. But even so. . . . (*She
looks through the book*.)

FLISS: Gwenda, is there anything
breakable in this bag?

GWENDA: Did you see the film? I loved
the music. (*She sings the* Dr Zhivago
theme.) What was his name? You
know the one, he's rather good at
cards.

FLISS (*drops bags and throws down box;
there is a tiny breaking sound as if
breakables were in the bag*): Omar
Sharif, and he's a compulsive gambler.

GWENDA: Oh the poor man! Is he
having treatment?

FLISS: I expect he's having a ball. It's
only a problem when the money runs
out.

GWENDA: Do you know him?

FLISS: No, but we did compulsive
gambling at college last week. It's all
tied up with orgasm.

GWENDA: Lack of?

FLISS: Well of course lack of, it's
compensation.

GWENDA: Surely not in his case, Fliss!
He's such an attractive man!

FLISS: To you he might be, to me he's
a boring old Egyptian fart.

GWENDA: You're so unkind, Fliss. So
uncharitable.

FLISS: I save my charity for those
deserving it.

GWENDA: I don't understand why you
want to be a social worker. You don't
seem to like anything or anybody,
apart from dirty old tramps and
delinquent Rastafarians. You'll end up
catching a contractable disease from
one or the other of them. You mark
my words.

FLISS *laughs.*

And here's me who absolutely adores
people in crisis and I can't even get on
the Social Work Training Course. It's
so unfair!

FLISS: You do it because you want to
do it.

GWENDA: I do it because these poor
women need me. There's something in
my personality that they respond to.

FLISS: It's the fellowship that one
hunted animal feels for another.

GWENDA: What do you mean by that?
I'm not used to people who speak in

riddles. Some of us missed university unfortunately.

FLISS: Unfortunately I didn't.

GWENDA: So that's another thing you don't like. Your parents must be so disappointed in you.

FLISS: My parents are incapable of feeling any emotion; they're dead people.

GWENDA: Oh, I'm sorry, dear, I didn't know.

FLISS: I mean they live in Reading. I couldn't breathe when I lived at home. I was stifled.

GWENDA: I was asthmatic when I was a girl, I never once held a hockey stick or a netball. I just stood on the sidelines holding the armbands and blowing the whistle at half-time. (*She sighs with self-pity*.)

FLISS: Oh sod it! What's the point? (*She goes out angrily*.)

GWENDA (*unaware that* FLISS *has gone, she continues stacking the books into paperback and hardback piles*): I read a lot when I was a girl. Asthmatics are usually well-read, have you noticed? I had Enid Blyton's complete works. Complete. My father brought one home every Friday night without fail. My mother had a quarter pound of Mint Imperials, father had two ounces of Shag and I had my new Enid Blyton. I'm sure that's why I'm quite without racial prejudice you know. Golly, Wog and Nigger were always my favourites, they were naughty to the other toys, but they always took their punishment well. (*She finds* Black Beauty.) *Black Beauty!* I could go on *Mastermind* with *Black Beauty* as my main subject. (*Quickly*:) What was Black Beauty's mother's name? (*Carefully*:) Duchess. (*Quickly*:) Who was the first man to break Black Beauty in? (*Carefully*:) Squire Gordon. (*Quickly*:) What lesson did Squire Gordon teach Black Beauty? (*Softly*:) You must never

start at what you see, nor bite nor kick, nor have any will of your own. But always do your master's will, even though you may be very tired or hungry. That was more or less what father taught me. It's kept me in good stead, service first self second.

FLISS (*enters carrying more plastic bags and a standard lamp, the floral lampshade is on her head*): That's everything out of the car. (*She dumps the bag down*.)

GWENDA: Fliss! You look lovely in that lampshade, it really suits you. Look in the mirror.

FLISS: Don't be ridiculous, Gwenda. It's hideous.

GWENDA: No, really. It's the first time I've seen you in anything feminine. You're usually such a scruff-bag. Of course, I know it's *de rigueur* to dress *à la* bohemian at college but . . .

FLISS: Actually it isn't. (*She takes the lampshade off*.)

GWENDA: The ladies like to see us dressed well, it makes them feel secure.

FLISS: Has research been done on it?

GWENDA: I don't know, I expect the Americans have looked into it.

FLISS: I fail to see the correlation.

GWENDA: Well then I shall have to be blunt. (*She takes a deep breath*.) Felicity . . .

FLISS: Fliss.

GWENDA: If I were an agoraphobic who'd been shut in the house for years, I would not be tempted into the big wide yonder by somebody who looked like you!

FLISS: And I wouldn't be enticed out by somebody clad from head to foot in sodding man-made fibres!

GWENDA: Let's keep it on a professional level, Felicity. They're quick to dry and non-iron, they suit my life-style.

I'm a very busy woman. The polyesters have done untold service for women's emancipation. The denims might demonstrate but it's the bri-nylons in the background that enable them to.

GWENDA *starts to assemble the standard lamp. She is upset, her movements are jerky. It should be obvious that she is carrying on an internal dialogue.*

FLISS: I locked the boot. (*She hands* GWENDA *the keys.*)

GWENDA: I prefer the boot *unlocked.* (*They stare at each other.*) Disadvantage working-class criminals have forced their way into my boot twice. I've lost two jacks and a tin of Gum-gum. (*She takes a light bulb out of her bag.*)

FLISS: Well, I'll go and *unlock* the boot. (*Pause.*) Would you like me to open all four doors and turn the radio on?

GWENDA: No thank you. The car's interior is protected by technology.

GWENDA *hands the keys back and* FLISS *goes out.*

GWENDA (*sings*): Would you like your lamp on, Daddy? Is the pain bad? Nurse will be here soon. Daddy don't be sad. Please don't look like that, Daddy, don't apologise. I'm putting on your lamp now, Daddy. Close your eyes. (*She screws the light bulb in, switches the lamp on and looks at it.*) Yes, I'll ask three pounds for you.

FLISS (*enters*): Katrina's outside.

GWENDA (*in a panic*): Oh! Where?

FLISS: She's sitting in the car working up to an anxiety attack.

GWENDA: Is Maurice there?

FLISS: Of course, when is he not?

GWENDA: I'd better go to her.

FLISS: Oh give her a chance. The deal was that she'd walk unaided up the path and through that door. She knows you're here.

GWENDA: Is it a serious attack?

FLISS: It's hard to tell with Katrina isn't it? She's either giving an Oscar-winning performance as Our Lady of Lourdes or punishing Maurice for forgetting her *Woman's Own.* If I had my way, she'd be permanently wired up to a lie detector.

GWENDA: Oh yes? An expert on agoraphobia are you now, Felicity?

FLISS: Fliss.

GWENDA: Know all about it, do you?

FLISS (*through gritted teeth*): No.

GWENDA: No. But I do! Professional cowards, and it takes one to know one, I'm an ex-aggie myself.

FLISS: If I were a leper, I wouldn't want an ex-leper to treat me. I'd want a consultant in tropical medicine.

GWENDA: Who said anything about leprosy? I run a self-help group for agoraphobics.

FLISS: You can't call them a group. They've never met!

GWENDA: They're in telephone contact!

FLISS: I hope that oily-haired creep Maurice isn't staying.

GWENDA: He's been a tower of strength to Katrina. I don't know what she'd have done without him.

FLISS (*quietly*): I do.

KATRINA *enters. She leans on the door jamb. She is a pretty woman in her early thirties.*

KATRINA: Maurice says to tell you I'm having an anxiety attack.

GWENDA (*in a panic*): Katrina! Where's Maurice? Have you taken a pill? Sit down. (KATRINA *sits.*) Now start breathing! In . . . out . . . in . . . out . . . in . . . out . . . . Relax, relax!

FLISS: For Christ's sake, Gwenda, calm down!

GWENDA: Don't interfere, Felicity, carry on breathing, Katrina. In out, in out, in out, relax, float, float. Shall I sing your song?

KATRINA: No, don't bother. (KATRINA *escapes from* GWENDA.)

FLISS: Gwenda, she's all right.

KATRINA (*to* FLISS): Let her sing, it calms her down. (*She smiles.*)

GWENDA (*sings*): If you're happy and you know it, clap your hands.

KATRINA (*walks slowly around the room touching surfaces, accustoming herself to the strange environment*): She can't sing as well as I can. Did you know I was a singer?

FLISS: Yes, you told me.

KATRINA: When?

FLISS: I've been to your house a couple of times. I'm training to be a social worker.

KATRINA: Did you see my photographs?

FLISS: Yes, you showed them to me.

KATRINA: Did you see the one of me and Hughie Green?

FLISS: Yes.

KATRINA: I was a songstress.

FLISS: Sorry, I . . . ?

KATRINA: That's what they called me in the *Stage.* Have you heard of the *Stage?* It's a newspaper.

FLISS: Heard of it, yes.

KATRINA: I was nearly on *Crackerjack.*

FLISS: I'm very pleased you came today. Are you pleased?

KATRINA: No. I'd rather be at home.

FLISS: Why?

KATRINA: East west, home's best.

They both turn to GWENDA *who is finishing her song.*

GWENDA: There! It always does the trick. You look much better now, Kat.

Oh I do think you're a big brave girl coming here on your own. (*She hugs* KATRINA.)

KATRINA: I didn't come on my own. Maurice brought me in the car.

FLISS: But you walked up the path on your own, didn't you?

KATRINA: No, Maurice brought me to the door. (*To* FLISS:) I can't go out on my own. I'm an agoraphobic.

GWENDA: Has Maurice gone now?

KATRINA: No, he's waiting for me in case I have to go home. He's sulking because he's not allowed to come in.

GWENDA: Oh dear! I'd better have a word with him. Felicity will look after you. I'll only be in the car park if you need . . .

GWENDA *rushes out. There is a short pause.*

KATRINA: I can't stand her, can you?

FLISS: She's all right. She means well.

KATRINA: She's in love with Maurice.

FLISS: Is Maurice in love with her?

KATRINA: No. He doesn't like neurotic women. And anyway he loves me.

FLISS *drags out a trestle table.*

FLISS: And how do you feel about him?

KATRINA: Oh I can't *stand* him! (*She giggles nervously.*)

FLISS: Would you help me with this table.

KATRINA: Is it heavy?

FLISS: Quite heavy.

KATRINA: I'd better not, I'm not allowed to lift anything heavy.

FLISS *sets up the table.*

FLISS: Are you pregnant?

KATRINA (*loudly*): No! (*Normally:*) I don't like sex, do you?

FLISS: I like it very much.

KATRINA: I'm repressed. Gwenda and Maurice told me.

FLISS: What don't you like about it?

KATRINA: Ugh! Well everything! His horrible *thing*, the noises he makes. I don't like him twiddling my knobs. You know (*She holds her breasts.*) but worst of all is the wetness, ugh. And he's such a weight! I felt half squashed to death by the time he'd finished. I don't see why people rave about it. I'd sooner do a jigsaw.

FLISS: How does Maurice feel about it?

KATRINA: I don't know, I never ask him. We don't do it any more so it never comes up. (*Pause.*) He seems cheerful. (*Pause.*) He spends a lot of time in the bathroom.

GWENDA *enters nearly hidden under a pile of showbiz-style dresses. She carries an Elvis Presley mirror under one arm and a Hula-Hoop is hung round her neck.*

GWENDA: It's twenty-five past eleven already! I promised to pick the others up by half-past. (*She dumps the dresses.*) Where are my car keys? (*She stands still, trying to compose herself.*) Oh I'm so tired! I've been on the go since six; my Teas-made ejaculated prematurely.

FLISS (*handing over keys*): Drive carefully. Don't kill them all on their first day out.

GWENDA: Can you cope with Katrina? I won't be long. (*The Hula-Hoop is still round her neck.*)

FLISS: Hadn't you better leave the Hula-Hoop?

GWENDA (*at the door, passes mirror to FLISS; to KATRINA*): Oh! Maurice says if you need him, he'll be in Sainsbury's for the next hour, after that he'll be in the car wash, washing the car. He's written the numbers down. (*She pushes a scrap of paper into KATRINA's hand.*) Bye! (*She rushes out.*)

FLISS: How long is it since you were out of your house?

KATRINA *starts to rip up the piece of paper.*)

KATRINA: Without Maurice or Gwenda?

FLISS: Yes. In your street for instance.

KATRINA: Well, Gwenda's been visiting for two and a half years and I'd been in then for two so it's . . . Oh I don't know. (*She throws the pieces of paper over her shoulder.*)

FLISS: Yes you do, what's two and a half and two?

KATRINA: I don't like sums.

FLISS: For Christ's sake, that's not a sum! What's two and a half and two?

KATRINA: Don't shout at me!

FLISS: Add it up, go on. Two and a half and two.

KATRINA: You're shouting at me. I want to go home. Take me home.

FLISS: I can't take you home. I haven't got a car.

KATRINA: I don't like it here, I want to go home.

FLISS (*loudly*): How many years is it since you came out of your house?

KATRINA (*shouts*): Four and a half!

FLISS: Thank you. (*Pause.*) Are these your things? (*She indicates the dresses and mirror.*)

KATRINA: Yes. They're for the rummage. Elvis used to be the one but then Maurice told me that he was a drug addict and wore nappies and that. So he had to go. It's Barry now. He's my inspiration to get better. I want to see him in the flesh.

FLISS: Barry?

KATRINA: Yes. Ignorant people say he's ugly and laugh at his nose. But they're only jealous because he's rich and famous.

She pulls her jumper up to show her Barry Manilow T-shirt.

FLISS (*reading*): Oh! Barry Manilow the singer!

KATRINA: He's more than a singer! He's got a bigger fan club than he (*she indicates the crucifix.*) ever had. Still, if you're not a fan, you're not a fan.

Song about Barry Manilow.

FLISS *sets up the trestle tables. She speech-sings certain words.*

FLISS: Why don't you hang your dresses up? They'll crumple if you don't. The sequins will get bent.

KATRINA *hangs up the dresses.*

KATRINA: They were sewn on by hand you know.

FLISS (*ironic*): Really! How truly staggering.

KATRINA: Maurice made all my stage-wear. He's very good with clothes. He chooses everything for me. Well, nearly everything. He wouldn't buy me my T-shirt so I sent away for it. The milkman posted the letter. Maurice doesn't know I've got it. I keep it in my sanitary-towel box next to Barry's picture. I wear it on Saturday mornings when Maurice is at Sainsbury's.

GWENDA *enters carrying a plastic bag and men's suits on hangers. She has one arm around* BELL-BELL. BELL-BELL *is a very neat, middle-class Scotswoman. She is carrying two boxes, one is full of knick-knacks, the other full of musical instruments.*

GWENDA: Well, here we are. Safe and sound. This is Bell-Bell. (*To* BELL-BELL:) Do you remember Fliss? She's the social worker who came to your house.

KATRINA: She's not a proper one yet.

FLISS (*smiles*): Hello!

GWENDA: And this is your telephone pal, Katrina. Say hello to Bell-Bell, Kat.

KATRINA: Hello.

BELL-BELL: Hello.

GWENDA: Why don't you sit down next to Kat, Bell-Bell? You two must have so much to say to each other.

BELL-BELL *sits down on the piano stool.* KATRINA *gives her the once-over.*

FLISS: Where's Margaret?

GWENDA (*lying*): She wouldn't answer the door. I knocked until my knuckles were literally raw.

FLISS: But she promised she'd come! She was looking forward to it.

GWENDA: I think we were a little optimistic with Margaret. She's a mass of neuroses.

FLISS: But I phoned her this morning. She said she'd had her coat on since half-past seven.

GWENDA (*pleased*): There you are then, you see. That's not normal, is it?

FLISS: I'll go round and fetch her.

GWENDA: We've got to be ready for the public by two.

FLISS: It won't take long! Can I borrow your car?

GWENDA: No, I'm only third party.

KATRINA: You lent it to Maurice.

GWENDA: Maurice is a knight of the road.

FLISS (*losing patience*): She's sitting at home waiting for us.

GWENDA: But Margaret's so unpleasant! She'll only spoil things.

KATRINA: She's the one that swears, isn't she?

GWENDA: Yes, constantly. And I won't tolerate it in public.

FLISS (*angrily*): I'm going to fetch her! Are you going to lend me the car or not?

There is no reply.

Do you expect her to walk here?

GWENDA (*throwing keys at* FLISS): Don't turn your back on that car once!

FLISS *starts to leave.*

FLISS: Gwenda, I know you don't like Margaret but for Christ's sake make an effort will you? It's her first day out. She's been in longer than anyone else.

She goes out. The door slams.

KATRINA: She makes it sound as if she's been in prison. (*She laughs.*)

The WOMEN *stare at the door.*

I can't stand her, can you?

GWENDA (*grudgingly*): She's all right, she means well. She hasn't had our experience in life. It'll come in time.

KATRINA (*to* BELL-BELL): Are you the one who's husband is dead?

GWENDA: Don't remind Bell-Bell of her sad loss, Kat!

KATRINA: I won't, it's just that I thought she might be the one that's married to the Yugoslavian.

GWENDA: No! That's Ruby! She's gone back in. Bell-Bell's husband originated from the Shetlands, didn't he Bell-Bell?

BELL-BELL: The Hebrides.

GWENDA: That's right; I knew it was something to do with sheep.

KATRINA: Which part of England's that in?

BELL-BELL: The wet part.

There is a pause. BELL-BELL *plays a few notes on the piano.*

KATRINA: Are you having an anxiety attack?

BELL-BELL: No, I'm playing the piano.

KATRINA: You've got a limited range, haven't you? (*She laughs.*)

BELL-BELL: So have you.

KATRINA *crosses to* GWENDA.

KATRINA: Gwenda, I think I've just been insulted.

GWENDA (*cuddling her*): Don't be paranoid, Kat. Bell-Bell's only adjusting her perspectives. She's normally a very placid woman, aren't you, Bell-Bell?

There is no response apart from a spectacular piano rag played by BELL-BELL.

(*Shocked*): How were you able to do that?

BELL-BELL: Piano lessons. Two a week for nine years.

GWENDA: I've got a little tune I can play. Move along, Bell-Bell.

GWENDA *sits at the piano and plays 'Chopsticks' badly. When she's finished, she looks at* BELL-BELL *and* KATRINA *for approval, but both look steadily at her without speaking.*

What did you do with the children, Bell-Bell?

BELL-BELL: They're at Derek's mother's, watching *Tiswas* in colour.

KATRINA: You're black and white are you?

BELL-BELL: Yes, and proud of it.

KATRINA: Are you? I'd be ashamed to admit it.

GWENDA *crosses over and picks up* DEREK*'s suits.*

GWENDA: Are all these Derek's ex-things?

BELL-BELL: Yes.

GWENDA (*looking in boxes*): He seems to have been a man of taste judging by his consumer durables.

She picks over the wallet, shaving kit, travelling clock, gloves, binoculars etc.

BELL-BELL: Yes, he always bought things to last.

GWENDA: And in the end he was outrun by a quartz travelling alarm. (*She sighs.*) It's so sad.

KATRINA (*looking at binoculars*): How much are you going to charge for these?

BELL-BELL: I hadn't thought.

KATRINA (*looking through binoculars*): Oh they're ever so good. I can see all the blackheads in your chin, Gwenda.

GWENDA: You can't give Derek's belongings to a rummage sale, Bell-Bell, they're much too good.

BELL-BELL: It's time I got rid of them. He's not coming back, is he?

GWENDA: Not in this world no, but if I were you I'd hang on to them a bit longer. Until you're emotionally stronger.

BELL-BELL: I feel stronger now. I don't want to take them home with me again.

GWENDA: I'm sure I'm right, Bell-Bell, now put them back into the box.

KATRINA: You have to do as Gwenda says, she's in charge of us.

BELL-BELL: I don't want his things in the house any more.

GWENDA: Don't you think that's rather callous of you? He'd turn in his grave if he knew . . .

BELL-BELL: He was cremated.

GWENDA: Well his ashes would never settle. (*She opens the other box.*) Now you just can't give his musical instruments away!

GWENDA *takes out a mandolin;* BELL-BELL *takes it from her.*

BELL-BELL: They're not his, they're mine.

GWENDA: What a sly old thing you are. I didn't know you had any talents.

BELL-BELL: I used to play before I got married.

KATRINA: You don't look musical.

BELL-BELL: I don't play them much. It annoys the neighbours. The walls are so thin.

KATRINA: You're in a semi, are you?

BELL-BELL: Yes.

KATRINA: We're in a detached with a separate garage and mature garden.

GWENDA: And Bar-B-Q patio. Katrina's husband is a boutique owner.

KATRINA: He owns Katrina's Kabin in Shepherd's Bush. That's Kabin with a 'K'. Do you get it?

GWENDA: Clever isn't it?

KATRINA: Maurice could get you a good price for your instruments; he's still got connections in the business.

BELL-BELL: Maybe I should take them back home.

GWENDA: No, Katrina's right. We'll let Maurice cast his semi-professional eye over them first.

BELL-BELL *strums the mandolin.*

GWENDA: Do you mind, Bell-Bell? I've got an aversion to stringed instruments.

BELL-BELL *stops playing.*

I wonder if Maurice could get into Derek's suits?

KATRINA (*looking at suits*): Maurice wouldn't be seen dead in anything like these! He likes things with charisma.

GWENDA: Well you've certainly had a clear-out of Derek's belongings, Bell-Bell.

BELL-BELL: I'll be needing extra room in the wardrobe soon. I've sent away for a fun fur.

GWENDA: Oh! But what do you want a fun fur for? You never go outside. You're an agoraphobic.

BELL-BELL (*defensively*): I go to the dustbin and back.

GWENDA: Well, I suppose you must get your fun where you can.

GWENDA *turns and shepherds* KATRINA *over to the shoebox; they pair up old shoes.* BELL-BELL *sings her fun-fur song.*

After the song:

KATRINA: Have another go.

Reprise of song. KATRINA *joins in with a tambourine and does a flamenco-type dance. She enjoys showing off her talent.* GWENDA *watches* KATRINA *fondly.*

GWENDA: Oh, while we three are together (*Conspiratorially:*) don't take too much notice of Felicity. She means well of course but she's got a lot of untried modern ideas about treatment.

BELL-BELL (*eagerly*): Is there a new treatment?

GWENDA: No, of course not, nothing that works. I'd know about it if there was.

BELL-BELL: But would you tell us?

GWENDA: Of course, (*Pause.*) if I thought you were ready.

BELL-BELL: I'm ready now, Gwenda, would you take me to the doctor's on Monday? I want to talk to him about my treatment.

KATRINA: What treatment?

BELL-BELL: Well that's just it, I'm not having any.

GWENDA: Bell-Bell, you know how overburdened Dr Patel is!

BELL-BELL: I've been on tranquillisers since Derek died. It's time I got off them.

KATRINA: I've been on them four and a half years and they've not done me any harm. (*She gives a vacant look.*)

GWENDA: Yes. They're extremely effective on naughty children and unhappy women.

BELL-BELL: I don't know if I'm unhappy any more and I won't know until I stop taking them.

GWENDA: But if you don't use your clothes prop, what happens to the washing line?

BELL-BELL *and* KATRINA *stare blankly at each other.*

KATRINA: I don't know, Maurice does the washing.

GWENDA: It sags doesn't it? Ergo — we all need our prop and support. I'm very fortunate in having the Lord as mine. I do wish you'd give yourself up to the Lord, Bell-Bell. Katrina has.

KATRINA: He was very pleased when I joined, wasn't he, Gwenda?

GWENDA: He was over the moon, Kat. I was cured by spiritual healing, did I tell you Bell-Bell?

BELL-BELL (*sarcastically*): Yes I think you mentioned it in passing. A million times or so.

GWENDA: I was inside for years looking after Daddy. The doctors said he mustn't be left alone for one minute. They said that he could go at any time.

KATRINA (*sings*): Tell me the old story.

GWENDA: Katrina, I'm trying to talk! So naturally I did what any good daughter would do in the circumstances; gave my little job up. The girls in the office presented me with a crystal sherry decanter. Oh there were tears all round the afternoon I left, and I must confess to feeling a little resentful myself. I did love my job.

KATRINA *mouths a few words here and there. She has heard this story many times.*

Joan from the office called round a few times, but Daddy started to be rather difficult so she stopped coming. Then everyone stopped coming, it was just me and Daddy and the home help twice a week.

She drifts off into thought.

KATRINA (*to* BELL-BELL): The next bit is about when he died.

BELL-BELL: I know.

KATRINA *undermines* GWENDA's *story.*

GWENDA: Then the poor old chap passed on and I had to force myself to go outside to the funeral. I fell into the grave you know. The other mourners thought I was grief-stricken but it wasn't that, my legs simply gave way with the terror I felt at being outside again. The vicar was a very modern chappie, wanted to be called Les. He called round to see me the next day and I made him a cup of Bovril. Then he stood up and said, 'Gwenda, I can't keep my hands off you, you're crying out for the touch of the Lord.' And I went down in front of him and he stroked my face and my neck and my shoulders and I felt this strange glow inside me, then I was racked by the most joyful physical sensation, and all at once I felt free.

KATRINA: It sounds to me as if the vicar touched you up.

GWENDA: It was nothing like that! Nothing! Besides he was a card-carrying homosexual.

BELL-BELL: Maybe you felt free because your father died.

GWENDA: What an extraordinary thing to say! I loved Daddy more than life itself. No, I was spiritually healed. Dear Les. He's in Soweto now, the natives adore him.

KATRINA: Not long to go now – his brain went.

GWENDA: Daddy left his money to the Queen Mother, but Clarence House wrote to our solicitor and graciously gave it back to his next of kin, which was me. I decided to devote myself to the poor and ignorant . . .

KATRINA: Cheek!

GWENDA: . . . as a sort of memorial to Daddy.

BELL-BELL: And you turned to religion?

GWENDA: Oh, I could no more do without my religion than I could do without my continental quilt. (*Coaxingly*:) Bell-Bell, let me lay my hands on you.

BELL-BELL (*firmly*): No thanks. No mumbo-jumbo. That sort of thing doesn't last. I want to get out and stay out.

GWENDA: How about you, Kat?

KATRINA: It didn't work last time.

GWENDA: But I'm getting better all the time, Kat. Yesterday I found a broken-winged sparrow on my compost heap and do you know, within half an hour of my stroking its little fluttering wing, it had flown away over Acton as if it had never had a day's illness in its life.

KATRINA: All right you can do it, but don't press down so hard this time.

KATRINA *kneels in front of* GWENDA *who throws back her head in rapture.* GWENDA *lays both hands on* KATRINA's *head.*

GWENDA: Dear Lord. Thank you for allowing Katrina and Bell-Bell to leave their homes. They beg forgiveness for their sins . . .

BELL-BELL: I certainly don't. (*She busies herself with rummage.*)

GWENDA: I speak to you as a dear friend, a Christian, one of a despised minority. Yes, I'm a Christian, Lord and I'm proud of it, Lord.

BELL-BELL (*ironic*): Hallelujah!

KATRINA: Yes, Hallelujah!

GWENDA: I'm no last-minute, death-bed convert.

BELL-BELL: No, Sir!

GWENDA: I'm a twenty-four hour, round-the-clock Christian!

BELL-BELL: Yes, Siree!

GWENDA: And Katrina's trying, Lord, she's trying.

BELL-BELL: She's very trying, Lord.

KATRINA: Bell-Bell! This is *my* prayer!

BELL-BELL *laughs and turns back.*

GWENDA: Heal her, Lord, heal her. Free her from this curse. Send down your all-powerful love.

KATRINA: Oh Barry!

GWENDA: Enfold her in your all-powerful arms.

KATRINA: Barry, take me in your arms.

GWENDA: Fill her with your love.

KATRINA: Fill me, Barry.

GWENDA: Take possession of her, Lord!

KATRINA: Possess me, Barry, possess me!

GWENDA: I can feel it coming, Kat!

She makes one last effort as if passing a huge turd.

KATRINA: Gwenda! You're pulling my hair!

FLISS *enters and crosses to* BELL-BELL.

FLISS: What's going on?

BELL-BELL: Spiritual healing.

FLISS: Acton's answer to Saint Francis of Assisi. (*She giggles.*) Gwenda! Gwenda!

GWENDA (*with a shuddering sigh, her body limp, arms hanging*): I'm sorry, Kat. It's no good I can't concentrate, not with an atheist in the room.

FLISS: Gwenda, come and help me with Margaret. She can't get out of the car, she says her legs have gone.

GWENDA: Then you'll have to take her home, we haven't got time to look after invalids.

FLISS: She'll be fine in a few minutes, she's just worked herself up into a state.

GWENDA *doesn't move.*

Come on, Gwenda! She's feeling sick and she's sitting in your car, on your sheepskin seat covers!

GWENDA: She's causing trouble before she's stepped foot in the place and we were having such a lovely time.

FLISS *and* GWENDA *go out. A siren is heard.* KATRINA *and* BELL-BELL *stand at the door and look out.*

KATRINA: Have you met Margaret Gittings?

BELL-BELL: Not face to face. We ring each other up.

KATRINA: Why don't you ring me up?

BELL-BELL: I do, sometimes. Your phone's engaged a lot.

KATRINA: I know, I ring dial a disc until I've learnt the words.

Pause. BELL-BELL *looks out of the door.*

BELL-BELL: What did you think of the streets?

KATRINA: What streets?

BELL-BELL: The streets outside.

KATRINA: I didn't look at them, I counted Maurice's dandruff instead. He makes me sit in the back of the car in case we have an accident.

BELL-BELL (*quietly*): The streets are awful — awful. I don't know how people can bear to walk about in them.

There is laughter offstage, shouts, then GWENDA *and* FLISS *enter carrying* MARGARET *between them.* KATRINA *sits down on the piano stool. She turns her back.* MARGARET *is a working-class woman. She has a loud voice and an assertive manner.*

MARGARET: Which one is Bell-Bell?

BELL-BELL: It's me.

MARGARET: Me bastard legs have gone, Bell-Bell. Thought I was doing all right.

GWENDA *raises her eyebrows.*

Put me down then!

FLISS: Where do you want to be?

MARGARET: Floor'll do.

They put her down under the crucifix. She lies on her back, then sits up and sees the crucifix.

Christ Almighty, look at that! Puts the fear of God in you, don't it?

GWENDA: It's meant to.

MARAGARET: Well, I did it! I bleedin' well did it!

GWENDA: Did what?

MARGARET: Well, I did it! I bleedin' (*She starts to break down.*) I ain't been further than putting the milk bottles out for bleedin' years. Now here I am, half a mile away, at a bleedin' rummage sale. (*She tries to control herself.*)

BELL-BELL: I'm glad to see you, Margaret. I couldn't have come without you.

MARGARET: Don't start me off, Bell-Bell. (*She cries.*) She always starts me off she does. It's a wonder I ain't been electrocuted before now. I only have to hear her voice on the phone and I'm off.

KATRINA: Phones don't run on electricity.

MARGARET: You're Katrina, ain't you?

KATRINA: What if I am?

MARGARET: You look like Shirley bleedin' Temple.

GWENDA: Can you get up now, Margaret? We need the floor.

MARGARET: You ain't selling the floor-boards, are you? (*She laughs.*)

GWENDA (*to* FLISS): What did I tell you?

FLISS (*laughing*): See if you can stand up, eh?

BELL-BELL *and* FLISS *help* MARGARET *up until she stands with their support.*

MARGARET: I can't yet, not on my own. Put me down on a chair.

FLISS: Gwenda.

GWENDA: What?

FLISS: A chair.

GWENDA (*fetching a chair*): Paralysis is quite common amongst hysterics.

MARGARET: Who's hysterical?

GWENDA: You are.

MARGARET: Balls! If anybody's hysterical, it's you.

GWENDA: I am *not* hysterical!

MARGARET: Well you make me laugh. (*She laughs loudly.*)

GWENDA: Are you going to sit around all day?

MARGARET: I hope not, I want to have a good look through the rummage, get myself a new winter wardrobe together. Specially now I'm making public appearances. (*She looks at* KATRINA*'s show-biz dresses.*) Them Shirley Bassey dresses for sale?

KATRINA: Only to good homes. They've been all over the country those dresses.

GWENDA: But it's time you let them go, isn't it, Kat? After what happened in Leicester.

MARGARET: What happened in Leicester?

KATRINA (*alarmed*): Gwenda, don't!

KATRINA *and* GWENDA *look at each other.*

MARGARET: 'ere Fliss, will you bring my stuff in?

FLISS: Yes. Katrina and Bell-Bell can help me. Come on.

KATRINA: We can't go outside.

BELL-BELL: Is it just to the car?

FLISS: It's only a few yards.

BELL-BELL: Will you come with us?

FLISS: I'll walk to the car with you and you can walk back together.

BELL-BELL: All right.

KATRINA: I'm not going out there. (*She goes to* GWENDA.) I can only go outside with Maurice or Gwenda, nobody else.

GWENDA (*to* FLISS): It's early days yet.

FLISS: Four and a half years is not early days! Come on, Katrina, you'll be with me and Bell-Bell.

BELL-BELL: Isabel. (*She walks to the door.*)

FLISS: You're not coming, Katrina?

KATRINA: No.

BELL-BELL: Gwenda started calling me Bell-Bell, but it's not my name. It's Isabel.

FLISS *and* BELL-BELL *go out. There is a long pause.*

MARGARET: Why didn't you pick me up, Gwenda?

GWENDA: I knocked three times.

MARGARET: You're a bleedin' liar! I stood at my window all morning waiting and you didn't come. I sent our Darren out to look for you, thought you might have been hijacked. Why didn't you want me to come?

KATRINA: It's because you're a trouble-maker.

MARGARET: Look here, chocolate box, the only trouble I've caused for the last fifteen years has been to myself. I ain't been nowhere to cause trouble.

GWENDA: Until today.

MARGARET: Yeah, until today.

FLISS *enters carrying carrier bags.*

FLISS: Where did you get all these toys from Margaret?

MARGARET: They're my Darren's. 'e ain't touched 'em for years. He's a hard little bleeder, now. It's all Doc Martins and tennis ball haircuts now.

Still least he keeps himself clean. (*She sees* BELL-BELL *entering carrying a toy garage.*) Here's our Isabel! (*She slaps her legs.*) Come on you bleeders, move!

GWENDA: Would you like me to lay my hands on you?

MARGARET: No thank you, I ain't bleedin' Lazarus. It's only me nerves.

MARGARET *gets up to go to* BELL-BELL *and takes the garage off her.*

Congratulations, Isabel on having the bottle to get out there on your own.

BELL-BELL: It wasn't for long.

MARGARET: It's a start, innit?

FLISS: Well done, Isabel.

MARGARET: Have a fag, Bell?

BELL-BELL: I shouldn't — but I will.

KATRINA: It's no smoking in here by order of the church.

MARGARET (*turning notice back to front*): Well smoking's allowed now by order of me. (*She looks at the crucifix.*) He wouldn't mind, dead neurotic he was, if fag's 'ad been around when he was alive, he'd 'ave been on sixty a day.

GWENDA: Our Lord would not have allowed a cigarette to touch his lips. And he was *not* neurotic.

MARGARET: 'Course he was. Hearin' voices in his head. Wandering about in the bleedin' desert. They'd lock the poor bleeder up nowadays and give him electric shocks.

GWENDA: Margaret, as a practising Christian . . .

MARGARET: Well keep on practising, Gwenda.

GWENDA: I can't stand here and take that lying down! Our Lord —

MARGARET (*cutting in*): He's your Lord, not mine.

GWENDA: He'd be yours if you let him. We all need something.

MARGARET: Twenty fags and one good shit a day's all I need.

FLISS: Margaret!

MARGARET (*angrily*): Well, she's always on at me, always. I don't tell her what to think, do I? She's got one bleeder brainwashed — ain't that enough? (*Slight pause*.) An' if she tries to lay her hands on me one more time, I'm gonna lay my hands round her bleedin' neck.

KATRINA: That's a threat to your life, Gwenda.

FLISS: I don't think Scotland Yard need to know, do you Katrina?

BELL-BELL: We've got to get the sale ready, haven't we?

BELL-BELL *starts to put up the trestle table.*

MARGARET: I've had my say. It's better out than in, like farting.

KATRINA: You shouldn't talk about religion or politics or anything like that. It's bad manners.

MARGARET *helps* BELL-BELL.

MARGARET: Well I ain't come out after fifteen years to talk about the fucking weather.

GWENDA: Felicity, I can't stand in a room where obscene language is used. It makes me physically ill. I shall have to leave you in charge until I recover my equilibrium.

She puts her coat on.

MARGARET: Christ, you ain't on Librium 'n all are you, Gwenda? It's the blind leading the bleedin' blind, ain't it?

MARGARET, BELL-BELL *and* FLISS *laugh.*

FLISS: Don't be ridiculous, Gwenda, we need you to tell us what to do. None of us have run a Bazaar and Rummage before.

MARGARET: It's sixpence on the door ain't it, Gwenda?

GWENDA: Sixpence! Where have you been since decimalisation?

MARGARET: At home.

GWENDA: Sorry.

MARGARET: Don't matter. (*Pause*.) Come on then, let's get cracking! We're flogging rubbish to the poor, ain't we? Least we can do is set it out nice.

FLISS: So what do we do, Gwenda? You're the rummage sale expert.

GWENDA: If you'll gather round, I'll define your areas of responsibility. Felicity, you're academic, so you've got the literature section.

FLISS: Literature! You can't call this dog-eared crap, literature! (*She stacks books on the table.*)

GWENDA: Bell-Bell, or Isabel. Bell-Bell please pay attention! You're in charge of the bric-à-brac section.

BELL-BELL: What's that?

GWENDA: Bric-à-brac! Knick-knacks.

MARGARET: Give a dog a bone. This old man came rolling home. (*She laughs*.)

FLISS: Do you know what you're selling now, Isabel?

BELL-BELL: Is it all the hard things?

FLISS: Yes, apart from the hard porn, I'm selling that.

MARGARET *is riding on a child's tricycle,* BELL-BELL *takes a pair of rubber gloves from a bag and puts them on.*

GWENDA: Margaret, toys for you I think. Please keep still, I can't concentrate. Now, you'll need to check the jigsaws, I don't want to contravene the Trade Descriptions Act. If it says five thousand pieces on the outside of the box, then the public will expect five thousand pieces to be on the inside of the box. No more, no less.

MARGARET: Fuck me. I ain't counting the bleeders. I'll be here until pissing midnight if I do.

MARGARET *gets off the bike and stares moodily into a jigsaw box.*

KATRINA: What about me?

GWENDA: You can help me. We've got clothing.

KATRINA: Ugh! All the smelly things! Can't I just sell my own dresses?

GWENDA: All right. But decide how much to charge in advance. I don't want you haggling with the *hoi polloi.*

The WOMEN *start to dress their own bit of table.*

And a few rummage sale ground rules: Number one, beware of the dealers. They're quite easy to spot. They all drive Bedford vans and wear second-hand fur coats. Number two, thieves are everywhere. So our own handbags and coats are piled into a heap, then hidden under a chair.

The WOMEN*'s own coats are given to* GWENDA.

Rule three: do not quote low prices just because you feel sorry for them. The poor are the architects of their own misfortunes. Rule four: today you are representing the wider agoraphobic community. As such your behaviour and choice of language must be exemplary.

MARGARET: What's she on about?

FLISS: She wants you to stop swearing in front of the public.

MARGARET: Christ all bleedin' mighty! She'll 'ave us at pissing elocution classes next.

GWENDA (*raising her voice*): Rule five! You will also be given a float.

MARGARET: Why, we going swimming after? (*She laughs.*)

GWENDA: Fifty pence each in a saucer! Margaret! Are you listening?

KATRINA: Margaret, listen to Gwenda, she's highly experienced at rummage sales. She's kept a guide dog in Pedigree Chum for a year.

GWENDA: Yes. And I've supplied half a water hole to Zambia. Now, if anyone comes over queer, I've emergency supplies of tranquillisers in my handbag. This is the first time you've faced the public for many years and you may be shocked at their deterioration. But I would ask you that, if you feel hysteria mounting, please mention it to Fliss or myself before you make an exhibition of yourself.

Rummage sale opera. After the opera the WOMEN *take their places behind their own area of table.* GWENDA *looks at her watch and stands by the door as if to open it on the stroke of two.*

The opera:

ALL: One pound, two pounds, three pounds, four pounds, do you think, maybe I could ask for more? It's just that this one's ten p, that one's twenty-five and this one's torn so fifteen's plenty.

FLISS:
Beano, Dandy come in handy
When you're in regression.

BELL-BELL:
Plastic flowers last for hours
Cheery for depression

KATRINA:
Sequins, spangles, furs and bangles
Pretty compensation

MARGARET (*playing with toys*):
Dolly, teddy, getting ready
For a conversation

GWENDA:
Cardigans and panties
Dressing-gowns and hankies

Underskirts and trousers
Overalls and blouses

FLISS:
Kevin Keegan's Life and
How to be a Wife and
Ten of Enid Blyton
Kids have used to write in

BELL-BELL:
Candlesticks and toastrack

GWENDA:
Buttons off this old mac

MARGARET:
Action Man keeps falling
He's on his knees and crawling
Supposed to be a hero
His sex appeal is zero

GWENDA:
Denim jeans and shirts
Dirty mini-skirts
Stained and smelly knickers

MARGARET:
They must be the vicar's

FLISS:
Murder Mysteries, Katy Did
Little Sisters, A to Z
Barbara Cartland's here to see
If there's honey left for tea

MARGARET:
Rabbits, doggies, gollywoggles
Rubik Kubes and Kermit Froggies
Hula-Hoops and plastic crap
Made in Taiwan by a Jap

ALL:
Knives and forks and coloured chalks
Caps and coats and broken boats
To be offered to the poor
Pray they'll pour in through the door

GWENDA:
Guard the saucers with your life
Bell-Bell careful with that knife
Margaret take it seriously

KATRINA:
Gwenda, I'm sure I've caught a flea

FLISS (*looking at a statue*):
What a priceless piece of kitsch.

MARGARET:
It's horrible you stupid bitch.

There is a knock on the door.

COMPANY:
Door!
Oh!
No!
Help!

GWENDA *throws open the doors.*

ACT TWO

*It is just getting dark outside. The
rummage sale is over. Not much has been
sold. The standard lamp is still there. The
Elvis mirror and two of* KATRINA'*s
dresses have gone. Only one of* DEREK'*s
suits is left. The toy gun is still there,
together with the majority of the shoes,
clothes, books and bric-à-brac.*
   GWENDA *is mopping the floor and
sprinkling disinfectant around. She has
an expression of revulsion on her face.*
BELL-BELL *is standing at the open door
looking out.* KATRINA *is sitting reading*
Woman. MARGARET *is retching (off)
and* FLISS *is making soothing,
comforting noises (off).*

KATRINA: Close the door, Bell-Bell,
   you're letting the smell of the streets
   in.

GWENDA: Leave it open, Bell-Bell. If
   there's one thing I can't stand it's the
   smell of vomit from a neurotic
   stomach.

BELL-BELL: Do you think any more
   customers will come now, Gwenda?

GWENDA: You know, Margaret ought to
   be doing this. (*She swabs the floor
   furiously*.)

KATRINA: Nobody will come now,
   not now it's dark.

GWENDA (*getting angrier*): I ought to
   make *her* clean it up.

BELL-BELL: Shall I make her some tea?
   She'll have a nasty taste in her mouth.

GWENDA: She ought to have more
   control over her stomach.

KATRINA (*to* GWENDA): It's her
   nerves. (*To* BELL-BELL:) Milky
   and three sugars please.

   KATRINA *shivers, gets up and closes
   the door.*

GWENDA: There's nobody more highly-
   strung than I am. I'm a veritable
   Stradivarius, but I don't give into it.

(*To* BELL-BELL:) Strong and no
sugar.

BELL-BELL *goes out to the kitchen.*

KATRINA: You have nervous rashes
   instead, don't you, Gwenda?

GWENDA: I have discreet nervous
   rashes, Katrina. (*Pause*.) Margaret
   Gittings won't come to another
   of my public functions, she was
   shouting and bawling as if she were a
   continental stall-holder on Petticoat
   Lane.

KATRINA: People seemed to like her
   though, didn't they?

GWENDA: Well, there are people and
   people, aren't there? It was hardly the
   Marks and Spencer set, was it?
   Tattooed grandfathers, single parents,
   Alsatians, delinquents and maladjusted
   children. Hardly a discriminating
   public was it? Nothing of any taste
   was sold. (*She strokes the standard
   lamp*.)

KATRINA: That big coloured boy asked
   Bell-Bell if he could put a deposit on
   Derek's binoculars and pay her so
   much a week.

GWENDA: We call them blacks now,
   Katrina. You must get up to date with
   your terminology. You could cause
   offence.

KATRINA: Why have blacks got white
   palms, Gwenda?

GWENDA: It's something to do with the
   sunlight not getting to them in Africa.
   Though heaven knows, they have them
   outstretched enough over here. She
   didn't agree to his crooked suggestion,
   did she?

BELL-BELL *enters.*

BELL-BELL: No, I gave them to him.

GWENDA: Genuine Ox-hide binoculars,
   and you gave them away?

BELL-BELL: I wanted to. Can I have my
   gloves please?

GWENDA: He's probably scanning the streets of Acton looking for somebody to mug.

BELL-BELL: He won't see far, not in the dark. (*She goes out.*)

KATRINA: I can't stand her, can you?

MARGARET *and* FLISS *enter,* MARGARET *wiping her mouth on a tissue.*

FLISS: Now sit down and take it easy, you've been running around like a Trot in a Labour constituency.

MARGARET: It's not being used to people what does it. I enjoyed it, don't get me wrong. But it's after it gets me.

FLISS: It was noble of you to clean up, Gwenda.

MARGARET (*to* GWENDA): You should have left it. I'd have done it.

GWENDA (*martyred*): It's too late now isn't it? It's all done now, isn't it? We couldn't paddle around in a lake of vomit, could we?

MARGARET: Christ! It were only a few fucking Rice Krispies! (*Pause.*) Anyway that disinfectant smells worse than my puke.

GWENDA: I'm surprised you know what disinfectant smells like, Margaret. I didn't know it was a commodity you were in the habit of purchasing.

MARGARET (*offended*): Oh that's nice, innit? Choice that is!

FLISS: Calm down, Gwenda, c'mon, give me the mop. You can take it easy now that the rush is off.

FLISS *tries to take the mop but* GWENDA *resists.*

GWENDA: Rush! Twenty-five people and two Alsatians. I don't call that a rush. The working classes are getting so apathetic that they can't even stir themselves to come out to a rummage sale.

MARGARET: You're just pissed off 'cos no one wanted your poxy old lamp.

GWENDA (*still wrestling with the mop*): That was my father's lamp! He was sitting under that lamp when our Lord took him.

MARGARET: Pity he didn't take the bleedin' lamp, an' all then.

GWENDA (*throwing the mop*): I can take anything you throw at me, Margaret. But when you drag Daddy into the argument . . . a dear sweet old man . . .

She rushes out into the loo. Everyone watches her. She re-enters.

Has anyone got a tissue?

KATRINA: I have. How long will you be crying?

GWENDA: About five minutes.

KATRINA: You better have a few then.

She hands over some tissues.

GWENDA: Thank you, I shall always have you, shan't I?

GWENDA *goes out with tissues covering her face.*

KATRINA: I can't stand her, can you?

MARGARET: Bleedin' good riddance. The best thing she can do is piss off home.

BELL-BELL (*off*): Tea up!

BELL-BELL *enters carrying a tray with a teapot, milk jug, sugar bowl and five cups and saucers.*

MARGARET: Give it 'ere, Bell, I'll be mother, you can do the sugar.

BELL-BELL: Gwenda's in the lavatory making a funny noise. Is she ill?

MARGARET: Not ill so much as off her bleedin' head.

FLISS: The only thing we can do for her is to keep her tea warm.

MARGARET: How long's her old man been dead then, not recent is it?

FLISS *pours the tea,* BELL-BELL *polishes the spoons and passes the sugar.*

KATRINA: Not really, he died watching football in 1966.

MARGARET: Fulham supporter was he?

KATRINA: No, he was watching the World Cup on television and he had heart failure during the last four minutes. Gwenda blames Geoff Hurst for her father's death.

MARGARET: Remember that, Fliss? Nobby running round with his gums all bare, half the country pissed as newts. (*She is on her feet.*) England! (*Clap, clap, clap.*) England! (*Clap, clap, clap.*)

World Cup Song.

FLISS: Actually I didn't see the match, my father loathed football so he wouldn't have it on. The smug pig sat out in the garden listening to *Down Our Way*. Mummy and I went shopping in Reading. It was like a ghost town. I felt quite peculiar, not of the common herd.

MARGARET: Yeah, you can tell you were brought up proper, Fliss. You use nice words and say 'em in the right order.

FLISS: An accident of birth. Merely the coupling of a middle-middle-class sperm and a lower-middle-class ova. Result: Felicity Sarah Markington's birth is announced in the *Daily Telegraph*.

KATRINA: Just think, you could have been Margaret Gittings.

MARGARET: I ain't always been a Gittings. I changed into one. I took 'is name to stop the bleedin' neighbours talking.

FLISS: Who's name?

MARGARET: Darren's father.

KATRINA: I didn't know he had a father.

MARGARET: Well he weren't off Tesco's meat counter; he *had* a father. Our Darren took after the evil little git an' all. Got that same weasel face.

KATRINA: What a thing to say about your own little boy.

MARGARET: He ain't never been a little boy. He only come out of my womb to see what he could nick. Robbin' little bastard.

FLISS: Does Darren ever see his dad?

MARGARET: He'd 'ave a job. He's dead.

BELL-BELL: What did he die of?

MARGARET: He was digging a trench and it fell in on him.

FLISS: That's a bit heavy.

MARGARET: Not as heavy as it was for him.

Pause. MARGARET has shocked herself. BELL-BELL starts to laugh.

KATRINA: Oh you're really awful!

They all laugh.

MARGARET: Who's going to see how Gwenda is? Her tea's getting cold.

There is a pause as all the WOMEN wait for someone else to volunteer.

MARGARET: It's no good me going, she hates *me*.

BELL-BELL: I'm sure she doesn't *hate* you, Margaret.

MARGARET: Oh I don't mind, I have that effect on everybody. I could never keep a friend.

BELL-BELL: Don't say that, Margaret.

MARGARET: Just letting you know, Bell.

There is a pause as the TWO WOMEN glance at each other. Everyone drops their voice.

KATRINA: Gwenda's always crying, she has trouble with her hormones.

MARGARET: Well she wants to have 'em out then, don't she?

FLISS: You can't have them *taken out*. They circulate in the bloodstream . . .

MARGARET: Well *drained out* then.

FLISS: What does she find to cry about?

KATRINA: It's mostly how wicked the world is, that and her vacuum cleaner breaking down.

MARGARET: I reckon she's the one that's breaking down, only it'll take more than a new suction hose to get her right.

KATRINA: She's having treatment for it.

FLISS: Don't tell me she's on the happy pills.

KATRINA: No, she's having the electric shock. EEC.

MARGARET: EEC? Ain't that the Common Market?

KATRINA: No, it's a machine that they plug you into. It does something to your brain.

MARGARET: What?

KATRINA: I don't know. I'm not an electrician am I?

FLISS: It's ECT and no one knows how it works. Poor Gwenda, how often does she light up?

KATRINA: Once a week on Wednesday afternoons.

FLISS: I saw her last Wednesday, she said she'd been in convulsions, but I thought she meant a bloody good laugh.

MARGARET: Poor bleeder. She kept that quiet.

KATRINA: I was sworn to secrecy. She said if it ever got out, she'd be ruined in voluntary social work. She said they're a vicious, spiteful lot in charity work. She said she'd be thrown off all the committees. She's on a lot of committees you know. She does a lot for the British Limbless Ex-Servicemen.

FLISS: What does she do?

KATRINA: She takes them to the limb-fitting centre in her car. But they have to make their own way home. She believes that people should stand on their own two feet.

BELL-BELL, FLISS *and* MARGARET *laugh.*

KATRINA (*straight-faced*): I don't see what's funny about it.

MARGARET: Just 'aving an 'armless joke, Kat. (*She waggles a bent arm about, laughs, and chokes on her tea. She has her back patted.*)

KATRINA: You shouldn't laugh at Gwenda. She's worked very hard getting the rummage sale organised. All the arrangements, the posters, collecting the rummage, queuing up in the bank for the small money for the floats.

FLISS: Actually Gwenda didn't do any of those things. I did.

MARGARET: How d'you mean?

FLISS: Gwenda didn't want us to have a rummage sale at all. She rang the caretaker last week and cancelled our booking. I had a lot of hassle getting the room back from the Acton Morris Men. They practise in here on Saturdays.

MARGARET: Do you know what? I reckon she don't want us to get better. I reckon she wants to keep us in. She likes having us at home.

BELL-BELL: Ah, your mouth's running away with you again, Margaret.

MARGARET: She does! The poor cow wants to keep us to herself!

There is a pause. Then GWENDA *enters, red-eyed, snuffling and blowing her nose.*

GWENDA: Is that my tea? Oh dear, it's got a cold look about it. Now I don't want any fuss made of me, carry on as if nothing had happened. Oh, I meant to say before Margaret's outburst, we must be out by six o'clock.

She notices the WOMEN's *faces which are registering shock and surprise as each* WOMAN *realises the truth of* MARGARET's *last sentence.*

Goodness gracious me, what in heaven's name is wrong?

FLISS: Nothing, I think we're all a bit tired.

GWENDA: You look like conspirators. (*She gives a little laugh.*) What have you been plotting? (*Pause.*) Katrina, my pet, would you count our takings? Put the ten-pence pieces in piles of ten and collect the paper money together with this paperclip . . .

FLISS: She won't need a paperclip. We only took one five-pound note.

KATRINA: Can't somebody else do it? I'm not used to money, Maurice does all that for me. I don't even use a purse any more.

MARGARET: She's like bleedin' royalty our Katrina is.

BELL-BELL: Shall I count the money? I'd like to know how much we've taken.

GWENDA: Well actually, Bell-Bell I'd already got a little job for you. A nice easy little job cutting buttons off the shirts.

FLISS: What do you want shirt buttons for?

GWENDA: I'm making a collage of St Paul's Cathedral, I need the buttons for the clouds.

MARGARET: You count the money if you want to, Bell-Bell.

GWENDA *cuts buttons off the shirts.*

FLISS: Katrina, you can help me, you've hardly moved all afternoon.

KATRINA: I'm not used to moving. That's why!

MARGARET: Well it's time you bleedin' well did then, you lazy cow!

KATRINA: I'm not lazy. I hardly have time to draw breath.

FLISS: What on earth do you do all day?

KATRINA: Starting from when?

FLISS: From when you wake up.

KATRINA: Well at eight o'clock Maurice brings me my breakfast on a tray. I have half a grapefruit, a soft-boiled egg, toast soldiers, a cup of tea and a five-milligram Librium. Then when he's gone to work I listen to Terry Wogan. He sometimes plays one of Barry's records but he can never pronounce his name properly, he calls him Harry Banilow. Sometimes I think Terry does it on purpose. Then what do I do? Yes, so I get up and have a Sainsbury's bubble bath. Then I get out, cream my knees and elbows. Immac under my arms, put all my make-up on and do my hair. Then of course I have to choose what to wear. Well time's getting on so I go downstairs, he's done all the house-work but I have to water the plants. Then I sit and listen to Barry until Maurice comes home.

MARGARET: Bleedin' hell!

FLISS: Shush!

KATRINA: He's home at one o'clock. He has tomato soup and two slices of bread and I have a doughnut, a cup of coffee and a five-milligram Librium. No sooner that's done than he goes back to work and I have to have a sleep until he comes back at teatime. Then, while we eat our digestives Maurice tells me all the news; all about the riots and the muggings and the rapes and the old people being murdered (*More emotionally.*) and the blacks kidnapping white women and all the little kiddies that's molested by perverts and the animals that's tortured by teenagers and the multiple crashes on the motorways and how people have been trapped inside their cars and been burnt alive. (*She continues more normally.*) Well, when he's told me all the latest, I have a ten-milligram Librium and he cooks the dinner. (*Pause.*) Meat, two veg, gravy, tin of fruit and Dream Topping, let's say. Then Gwenda comes round and Maurice and her talk about how the country's going down the drain. Then it's cocoa, two Cadbury's Fingers, Mogadon and bed.

There is a long pause during which time a siren is heard.

MARGARET: Your Maurice is a fucking maniac!

GWENDA: Maurice is *not* a maniac!

KATRINA: And he's not a fucking one, not any more.

FLISS: Katrina, Maurice has been telling you lies.

KATRINA: No, I know it's true. He cuts bits out of the newspapers and puts them in his scrapbooks. You've seen his scrapbooks, haven't you, Gwenda?

GWENDA: Yes, they're meticulously kept.

KATRINA: It must be true. If it's in the papers, it must be true.

MARGARET: I wouldn't wipe my arse on the papers.

KATRINA: East west, home's best. Nothing can happen to you if you're inside, can it?

FLISS: Katrina, you're more likely to die choking on a digestive biscuit than being burnt to death in a motorway pile-up.

GWENDA: How ridiculous! You're just trying to frighten her.

KATRINA: Is it true that if you stop breathing for long, you die?

FLISS: Yes.

KATRINA: Awful isn't it? Sometimes I wake up in the middle of the night just to make sure I'm not dead.

MARGARET: You might as well be dead. You're already livin' in a coffin and Maurice is diggin' your bleedin' grave.

FLISS: And we all know who the undertaker is, don't we? (*To* GWENDA:) How could you have allowed this to go on?

GWENDA: What to go on?

FLISS: Why have you let Maurice terrify Katrina into staying at home?

GWENDA: She's happier at home. (*To the group:*) You all are. The streets aren't safe for women.

MARGARET: I wouldn't mind finding out for myself though. I ain't been out there on my own since Darren was born.

BELL-BELL: How old is he now?

MARGARET: He'll be fifteen in June.

Pause.

BELL-BELL (*in a panic*): I've got to get out soon. I don't want to be in for fifteen years.

FLISS: Well don't look to Gwenda for any help 'cause she's already said you're better off at home.

GWENDA: You lying filthy Red! You Socialist lefty-pinko-liberal-beatnik-Bennite! I knew you had militant tendencies. I spotted it the first time I saw you. Do Social Services know you're a Communist?

KATRINA: I've never seen a Communist before, not in the flesh.

FLISS (*to* KATRINA): I'm not a Communist, I'm apolitical.

GWENDA (*shouting*): A political what? Come on, out with it!

KATRINA: Must you shout, Gwenda? I've got a headache due in five minutes.

GWENDA: I've given the best years of my pre-menopausal life to these women. I visit daily —

MARGARET (*cutting in; to* BELL-BELL): She always comes in the middle of *Crossroads.* I missed the fire because of her.

GWENDA: Without me, Margaret, you would starve to death. Who is it brings your groceries every day?

MARGARET: I don't ask you to. My Darren could get 'em.

GWENDA: Your Darren is a kleptomaniac and is banned from every grocery store within a two-mile radius of Acton High Street!

MARGARET: Yeah well, the walk'll do 'im good, won't it?

GWENDA: What about you, Bell-Bell? Do you still want me to get your household cleaners from the cash and carry?

BELL-BELL: I've got enough Harpic to clean up the River Ganges, Gwenda.

GWENDA: Kat?

KATRINA: You can still come round to my house if you like, I never listen to what you say anyway, so you don't bother me.

FLISS (*kindly*): You've got too involved, Gwenda. It's the cardinal sin of social work. It's almost the first thing you learn on the training course.

GWENDA (*more to herself*): The Communists at Social Services stopped me doing any training. I told them straight at all my interviews. I said, what this country needs is more men like Daddy. Capital punishment in schools. Teenagers in the army, fathers working and mummies at home. I was a naughty girl too once but thankfully I had a daddy who wasn't afraid to use discipline. They were against me from the start. I distinctly saw one bearded revolutionary sniggering at my interview hat. (*Pause. Then she continues more emotionally, getting hysterical:*) It's you and your kind who have made this country what it is today. A country where no decent God-fearing woman can walk the streets without being molested. (*She cries and hangs onto the lamp.*)

BELL-BELL: She shouldn't have brought that lamp here, it reminds her of her father.

MARGARET: Tall and thin and wore a flowered hat, did he?

BELL-BELL *laughs.*

GWENDA: I can see I'm surplus to requirements here, so if you'll excuse me I'll make my way home. (*She puts her coat on with jerky movements.*)

KATRINA: What about me?

GWENDA: What about you?

KATRINA: You can't leave me here.

GWENDA: It's quite clear where your affections lie now, Katrina. I've been tossed aside like a withered lettuce leaf, all that I ask is that you allow me to go with dignity. (*She falls over the mop.*) Goodbye!

FLISS: Don't be so bloody melodramatic, you can't leave us here with all this rummage.

GWENDA: You've staged a successful *coup d'état*, Felicity, and now like all revolutionaries you are left with the problem of who is going to attend to the drains.

GWENDA *leaves. The group quietly panics.*

MARGARET: What bleedin' drains?

FLISS: She was speaking metaphorically.

MARGARET: What?

FLISS: She was using a metaphor to illustrate a point.

There is a pause.

MARGARET: Well I ain't cleaning no bleedin' drains.

KATRINA (*to FLISS*): Are you in charge of us now?

FLISS: No.

BELL-BELL: Who is then?

FLISS: You're in charge of yourselves.

MARGARET: How we getting home?

FLISS: I don't know how you'll be getting home.

MARGARET: You're ditching us are you? A fine bleedin' social worker you've turned out to be.

FLISS: I'm not here as a social worker. I'm here as a student to see how a self-help group functions. I'm merely an observer.

MARGARET: If we'd known that we'd of had a whip-round and bought the bastard binoculars for you.

BELL-BELL: Somebody must be in charge of us.

KATRINA: We can't get home on our own.

MARGARET: And we can't stay here, the caretaker's locking up at six.

KATRINA: I could phone Maurice, is there a telephone near here?

FLISS (*irritably*): I don't know. Go outside and look for one.

MARGARET: What you being horrible for, Fliss? What have we done wrong?

FLISS: You've done nothing wrong, Marg. But I'm not getting saddled with running your lives, I haven't got the time.

BELL-BELL: Just help us to get home.

FLISS: It won't stop there, will it? It'll be Fliss, fetch my family allowance, or Fliss, pick up my prescription, or Fliss, pay my rent. I can't do it. Look, you wouldn't let yourselves bloody starve, would you? If you *had* to, you'd get to the shops.

MARGARET: Are you saying pull yourselves together?

FLISS: No, social workers are not allowed to say that. But you've got to face up to it sooner or later.

BELL-BELL: Face up to what?

FLISS: Whatever it is that's keeping you in.

KATRINA: We know what it is, it's agoraphobia.

FLISS: That came second, what came first?

A con brio choir sings offstage. Music.

There is a long pause as each WOMAN *finds something to do.* BELL-BELL *starts to count money,* KATRINA *starts to repack books into boxes,* MARGARET *starts to fold clothes.*

FLISS: Margaret!

MARGARET: I don't know any more. I can't remember anything.

BELL-BELL: She's been on Librium for fourteen years.

MARGARET: Fifteen.

KATRINA: I've only been on it for four and a half years.

BELL-BELL: I'm not on it at all.

KATRINA: You are brave!

The WOMEN *start dismantling the tables and packing the rummage.*

BELL-BELL: I'm on Valium instead.

KATRINA: Valium and Librium. Go together nicely, don't they?

MARGARET: Like Dandelion and Burdock.

KATRINA: 'Cept you don't get money back on the bottles. (*She laughs.*)

MARGARET: Wish you did. I'd be a fucking millionairess. (*She laughs.*)

FLISS: What would you spend the money on?

MARGARET: I'd go round the world.

KATRINA: Oh I wouldn't. I'd go somewhere nice.

FLISS: How can you go round the world if you can't go to the end of your street?

MARGARET (*in a raised voice*): You seen my street?

FLISS: Why don't you move?

MARGARET (*shouting*): Because, Felicity Sarah Markington from Reading, I ain't got no money and the council won't give me a transfer and I'm shit scared every time I put my nose out of doors.

FLISS: So you don't like where you live?

MARGARET: Who would? It's a shit hole.

FLISS: It's urban decay.

MARGARET: What's that?

FLISS: That's what you live in.

MARGARET: Sounds like a tooth disease.

FLISS: Well it's not, it's a building disease. But most people at least function in it. In as much as they can go from A to B.

MARGARET (*shouting*): What are you talking about?

FLISS: I'm trying to find out why you're scared.

MARGARET (*shouting*): I don't know why!

FLISS: Don't shout. Why are you always shouting?

MARGARET (*shouting*): Because no bleeder takes no notice of me unless I do!

FLISS: I'm trying to empathise with you. (*She shouts.*)

MARGARET (*shouting*): I don't know what you're talking about!

FLISS: I give up.

MARGARET (*quietly*): That's better, I understood that.

There is a pause.

FLISS: Don't you want to get better?

MARGARET: I don't know where to begin.

FLISS: Open the door and take two steps outside.

MARGARET: You know I can't do it.

KATRINA: Not in the dark!

FLISS: Darkness is a scientific phenomena, Katrina. It is not a veil of evil dropped on half the world. Go on, two steps, two measly little steps. Then you can come back inside.

MARGARET: Will you leave the door open?

FLISS: Yes.

MARGARET *goes to the door, opens it and looks out. The others watch her. After a pause* MARGARET *hurries back into the room and sits in a far corner.*

MARGARET: I ain't dressed right for going out at night am I?

FLISS: For Christ's sake, Margaret, you're just procrastinating.

MARGARET: No I'm not. I'm putting it off until I'm dressed right.

FLISS: You're only going a yard away.

KATRINA: Shall I get you dressed to go out?

MARGARET (*evasively*): No, it's all right, don't bother.

KATRINA: Oh let me! I know all about dressing up. What did you used to wear when you went out at nights?

MARGARET: Well, I'd put me best coat on.

KATRINA: What about dancing or nightclubs?

MARGARET: What about 'em?

KATRINA: What did you wear?

MARGARET: Nothing.

KATRINA: Nothing?

MARGARET: No, I never went to places like that.

KATRINA: So you've never had lamé next to the skin?

MARGARET: No.

KATRINA: Never had a frou-frou underskirt on and wobbled when you walked?

MARGARET (*scornfully*): Piss off.

KATRINA *fetches a glamorous dress.*

KATRINA (*excited*): Oh Margaret, now's your chance. Oh I've always wanted to do this, just like they do in *Woman*.

It's only clothes, make-up and hairdos, Margaret. Even *I'm* quite ordinary when I'm bare and naked. Try 'My Way' on.

MARGARET: What's 'My Way'?

KATRINA: This! I used to change into it for my big number. I had flowers thrown on the stage at the Leicester Boot and Shoe, that was a night to remember. It was in the Hawaiian Lounge and they had this fountain spurting water and a real plastic palm tree with real plastic pineapples on it. I got a standing ovation. Then somebody fell in the fountain and a fight broke out. All my dresses had names. Go on, put 'My Way' on.

MARGARET: No, I'll look pissin' stupid in it, won't I?

KATRINA: No, you won't.

MARGARET: I will here won't I? It ain't exactly Las Vegas, is it?

FLISS: Go on, Marg. It'll please Katrina.

MARGARET *starts to undress self-consciously.*

MARGARET (*laughing at* FLISS): It's you who needs doing over, look at the state you're in! You look like a bag of shit tied in the middle.

Female screams come from outside. The WOMEN *stand quite still, terrified. They turn and look at* FLISS *who rushes to the door leaving it open.* BELL-BELL *rushes to the door and slams it shut. The* WOMEN *watch the door. The screams turn into high-pitched, shrieking laughter. The* WOMEN *relax a little.* FLISS *comes back in, puffing.*

FLISS: Only kids playing about on the gravestones.

MARGARET: I thought some bleeder's throat was being cut.

All the WOMEN *laugh and relax.*

FLISS: Come on then, Marg.

MARGARET *undresses.*

KATRINA: I'm going to Las Vegas one day. It's my ambition. I've got the talent, Maurice says. He's making me some really amazing dresses. I haven't seen them yet. He keeps them at the Kabin but he says they're amazing, really amazing.

FLISS: I bet.

MARGARET: Don't look at my bra – it's got a safety pin in it. Where do all these bits and pieces go?

KATRINA: Come here! I'll do you up. (*She fiddles with the zips.*)

MARGARET: What do I look like, Fliss?

MARGARET *stands in the dress and clumpy shoes.*

FLISS: You need shoes. What size do you take?

MARGARET: Four and a half, or fives.

FLISS *rummages around in the shoe pile.*

KATRINA: Sit down, I'll do something with your hair. It looks like a Brillo pad that's been left in soak.

MARGARET *sits down and* KATRINA *fusses with her hair, taking pins out of her own.*

Bell-Bell, pass my make-up bag out of my handbag.

MARGARET: I don't want that shit on my face.

KATRINA: Margaret, your pores are crying out for something. Be quiet, I know what I'm doing.

BELL-BELL *passes her the make-up bag.*

Now, carry on backcombing, Bell-Bell.

FLISS *finds a pair of old stilletos and puts them on* MARGARET. KATRINA *makes up her face.*

MARGARET: I feel like a bleedin' human sacrifice.

KATRINA: Keep still. Stop wriggling around.

BELL-BELL: You're coming on nicely, Margaret.

FLISS: You're very clever with feminine artefacts, Katrina. Did you have any training in transformation?

KATRINA: No, it just came naturally to me. I've never climbed a tree in my life.

MARGARET: How much longer?

KATRINA: Open your mouth, I'm putting your mascara on.

MARGARET *opens her mouth.*

MARGARET: 'Ere careful! You nearly 'ad my eyeball on the end of that stick.

KATRINA (*indignantly*): Stick! It's called a wand!

MARGARET: Is that why I'm feeling like a fucking fairy?

KATRINA: You've got good long eyelashes, Margaret, do you do anything with them?

MARGARET: Open an' shut 'em, that's all.

KATRINA: What a waste! I've had to wear falsies since I was sixteen. Maurice said my eyelashes had no impact over the footlights. Right, now for the pulse points.

KATRINA *sprays perfume on* MARGARET.

MARGARET: Leave it out, Katrina! I smell like a one-woman knocking shop!

KATRINA (*shocked*): This is Chanel Number Five. You won't find this on any old pulse points. They're very fussy who they sell it to. You have to know somebody.

MARGARET: Have you finished?

KATRINA: Yes, you can stand up now.

MARGARET *stands, wobbling on the high-heels, round-shouldered and self-conscious.*

BELL-BELL: I don't know you, Margaret.

KATRINA: Margaret, stand up straight, push your knobs out.

MARGARET *attempts to.*

KATRINA: Like this.

She *assumes a showbiz pose.*

MARGARET: I can't do it, I ain't built like you.

KATRINA: Of course you can. Now walk round like this.

KATRINA *makes a showbiz entrance.*

MARGARET: What for?

KATRINA: You're going to make a big entrance in front of the public soon. Bell-Bell play us some music, do you know 'My Day'?

BELL-BELL *sits at the piano and plays 'My Day'.* KATRINA *and* MARGARET *sing.* MARGARET *gets a kick out of flouncing about in the dress.*

At the end of the song FLISS *opens the door, points to* MARGARET, *then points to the door.* MARGARET *walks to the door, hesitates, then walks out looking to left and right. She takes two steps forward, then walks backwards into the hall. The* WOMEN *cheer and shout.*

MARGARET: It were only two bleedin' steps.

MARGARET *sits down looking pleased with herself.* KATRINA *passes* MARGARET *a tissue.*

Get us me fags, Kat.

FLISS: Well done, Marg. Did you have a good time out there?

MARGARET: Don't know — I had me eyes shut.

KATRINA: You've got me to thank for that. I improved your self-image.

MARGARET: Bleedin' hell, Kat.

BELL-BELL: You did awful well, Margaret.

MARGARET: I know, I'm doing it again tomorrow.

Pause. MARGARET *lights a fag.*

BELL-BELL: We made nine pounds thirty-seven and a half pence.

KATRINA: Freddie *will* be pleased.

BELL-BELL: Freddie who?

KATRINA: Freddie Laker. Gwenda's sending him our rummage sale money. Didn't she tell you?

FLISS: I'd sooner throw it down the bloody drain.

BELL-BELL: What shall I do with the money, Fliss?

FLISS: Give it to the caretaker and tell him Gwenda owes him sixty-two and a half pence for the hire of the room. We made a loss.

MARGARET: Ten pounds for this poxy hole? It ain't worth that to buy it.

KATRINA: We've still got things to sell. The rummage isn't over yet. I've not bought anything yet.

FLISS: You haven't got any money on you, have you?

KATRINA (*thinking*): Oh no. Margaret, do you want to buy 'My Way'?

MARGARET: How much is it?

KATRINA: Sixty-two and a half pence.

MARGARET: It don't fit properly does it?

KATRINA: I could always get Maurice to alter it. He's very good with awkward figures.

MARGARET: I had a good figure before Darren was born.

BELL-BELL: Was he a big baby?

MARGARET: No, he was a little runt like his dad. But he damaged me somehow. I ain't been the same person since I had him.

FLISS: Did you want him?

There is a pause. A long siren sounds.

MARGARET: No! And I didn't want his dad neither. I had 'em both forced on me.

KATRINA: You could have said no. I do.

MARGARET: I did say no.

BELL-BELL: Oh dear.

BELL-BELL *moves away.*

FLISS: How old were you?

MARGARET: Eighteen and three days. I'd never seen a man's cock before. Hard to believe ain't it? So when it come poking out of his trousers I thought he'd got a banana in his hand. Then I twigged and tried to get to the door but he stood with his back to it.

BELL-BELL: I don't want to hear any more.

BELL-BELL *gets up and goes to the door.*

KATRINA: I do. I like anything like this.

FLISS: Shut up! Go on, Margaret.

MARGARET: He said, 'Lie down and take your drawers off.' He was only a little runt. I could have floored him, smashed his face in, but I didn't. He knew I was scared, see. So I laid down on the bathroom floor and he fiddled around with me and grunted like a pig and when it hurt me, he put his hand over my mouth. I could hear my old lady downstairs whipping a Yorkshire pudding. I could hear the chink of the spoon in the bowl.

BELL-BELL (*upset*): She should have used a wooden spoon for Yorkshire pudding.

KATRINA: Did he go all the way?

MARGARET: No, he stopped when he got to my bleedin' backbone!

BELL-BELL: Don't joke about it, Margaret.

MARGARET: Sorry, Bell. I could hear the kids playing and screaming outside in the street an' I thought, this isn't happening. Then he got off me, did his buttons up, took some change out of his pocket and threw half a crown on my belly. Then he went out. I heard him shout 'Tara!' to our mum. She shouted, 'Dinner'll be on the table at two o'clock sharp, Norman.' Then the front door slammed. I waited until his footsteps had died away and then I got up and looked in the bathroom mirror.

FLISS: What were you looking for?

MARGARET: A sign that would tell everybody what had happened. Then our mum called me down to peel the sprouts, so I went down after I'd washed. Our mum was like she always was Sunday dinnertime. Pissed off 'cos the men were in the pub and she was stuck at home with the fuckin' dinner.

FLISS: You didn't tell her?

MARGARET: No, our mum thought the sun shone out of his scrawny ass.

FLISS: Who was it?

MARGARET: It was somebody it shouldn't have been. I'll never tell who, never.

FLISS: And Darren was his baby?

MARGARET: Copped out first time. First and only. I didn't know see? So when I started putting weight on, I thought nothing of it. Then one of the girls says, 'You in the pudding club, Marg?' I says, 'Don't be daft, Vera, I'm Acton's last living virgin.' Because inside me I still was. I must have been five months gone by then. I gave up my job and told our mum I'd got the sack for nicking the laundry. She believed me 'cos every towel we had was stamped with the laundry's name. I stayed in bed most of the day after that. I was like an invalid, like a frozen invalid. Six weeks later I had him. I was reading the Sunday paper in bed. I had backache, then I had a pain so bad that my eyes turned inside out and he was there.

FLISS: What did you do?

MARGARET: I wrapped him in the *News of the World* and put him under the bed.

BELL-BELL: Wasn't he crying?

MARGARET: Him and me. I daren't look at him properly, I thought he'd be a monster like it says in the Bible. Then our mum shouts upstairs, 'Margaret, have you got that paper?' She comes up, pulls the paper out from under the bed and ages ten years in one second.

FLISS: Christ, Margaret. The *News of the World!*

MARGARET: He'll end up that way an' all, the rate he's going.

BELL-BELL: Why did you keep him?

MARGARET: You've had kids, Bell. You know what it's like.

BELL-BELL: My circumstances were very different, Margaret. We always did things properly, how they should be done.

MARGARET: It didn't do you no good in the end though, did it, Bell? You ain't got a bloke now, same as me.

BELL-BELL: I don't want another man. (*Pause.*) I only wanted Derek.

FLISS: How did Derek die, Bell, was he ill?

BELL-BELL *busies herself stacking teacups.*

BELL-BELL: He didn't die, he was made redundant. It was such a waste.

She turns her back.

MARGARET (*going to* BELL-BELL): Bell, you're wasting yourself staying in. You're a good woman, you should share yourself out.

BELL-BELL: I've got nothing to share. I only know how to keep a nice house. I give it a good clean through every day, windows, walls, floors, doors, furniture, carpets.

FLISS: What do you do when you've finished your housework?

BELL-BELL (*agitated*): There's no time for anything else. As soon as I've cleaned one surface, another one is dirty.

FLISS (*suspiciously*): What happens if you are interrupted, say if the telephone rings or somebody comes to the door?

BELL-BELL: Oh if that happens I have to start all over again.

FLISS: From scratch?

MARGARET *holds* BELL-BELL's *hand.*

BELL-BELL: Yes. I have to start off in the box-room, and I have to finish in the porch. It's just my way of doing things.

FLISS: Did you do this when Derek was alive?

BELL-BELL: Yes, he was very good, he changed before he came into the house and kept his feet on the newspapers.

MARGARET: What bleedin' newspapers?

BELL-BELL: The newspapers on the lounge carpet. (*Pause.*) I know it's not normal.

MARGARET: What happened when he was made redundant? Where did he sit all day — while you were cleaning?

BELL-BELL: He didn't tell me he'd been made redundant. (*Pause.*) He didn't tell me. I didn't know until I saw his boss at the funeral.

FLISS: How long was that?

BELL-BELL: Three months. He killed himself when his redundancy money ran out. He was very thoughtful, he did it in the bath so there wouldn't be much mess.

KATRINA: That was nice of him.

BELL-BELL: Liquid Gumption is very good on bloodstains.

MARGARET (*holding* BELL-BELL): Bell, we're a pair of headcases ain't we? But it don't mean we have to stay in all the time, does it?

FLISS (*trying to comfort*): You're not mad, Bell, you're just a bit neurotic.

MARGARET: You trying to cheer her up or what?

FLISS: It's normal to be a bit neurotic, nearly everybody's scared of something.

KATRINA: Maurice doesn't like spiders.

MARGARET: And you can't get our Darren into a lift for love or money.

KATRINA: What's Bell scared of then?

BELL-BELL: Germs!

MARGARET: Well you can't spend the rest of your life at home killing the bleeders.

FLISS: She won't have to — you're going out at least once a week from now on.

KATRINA: Where are we going?

FLISS: Christ knows, I'll find somewhere.

BELL-BELL: Are you going to give us treatment?

FLISS: I'm not. I'm not qualified and anyway I'm as neurotic as the next.

MARGARET: Why, what are you scared of?

FLISS: I break into a cold sweat whenever I see a semi-detached house.

MARGARET: So where do you live?

FLISS: Tower Hamlets.

The WOMEN *start the final packing away.*

MARGARET: You can have treatment the same time as us.

FLISS: No thanks. The thought of being able to see my parents again . . . ugh! (*She shudders.*) And that shrine of a house, those flowerbeds! Spring is a nightmare. Daffodils grow in clumps of six, no more, no less. The privet hedge is only allowed to flourish six inches above the fence. My God, the brutal way my father treats that privet, hacking at the leaves as if they are a battalion of Japanese. He doesn't garden, he controls. He spends so long in his greenhouse I expect him to take root in a bag of John Innes. Poor Mummy!

MARGARET: What's your old lady like?

FLISS (*trying to think*): I don't know, there was nothing there, nothing tangible. She sort of wandered around with a J Cloth in her hand desperately trying to anticipate my father's moods.

MARGARET: Do you go and see your mum and dad?

FLISS: No the suburbs are out of bounds for me. The sound of a lawnmower starts me off.

KATRINA: What do you start doing?

FLISS: Sweating.

MARGARET: Palms of your hands?

FLISS: Yes. And a sort of buzzing . . .

KATRINA: In your ears?

FLISS: Yes! Then I feel my legs going . . .

BELL-BELL: All weak and wobbly?

FLISS: Yes! And I think to myself, come on, Fliss pull . . .

KATRINA: Yourself together! But you can't, can you?

FLISS: No. And I feel sure I'm going to faint . . .

MARGARET: Right there in the street and that some bastard's going to look up your skirt and see your drawers?

FLISS: Well no, not exactly, Margaret.

MARGARET: You think you're going to spew up?

FLISS: Yes.

KATRINA: What about the shops, can you go into shops?

FLISS: Woolworth's is okay. Harrod's is out.

Agoraphobia song – 'Panic Attack' There is a terrific panic-stricken banging on the door.

MARGARET: It's the caretaker come for his bleedin' money.

FLISS *opens the door. A* WOMAN POLICE CONSTABLE *rushes in in a panic, then sees the* WOMEN *and becomes officious.*

WOMAN POLICE CONSTABLE: I saw the light on.

FLISS: Is it against the law?

WOMAN POLICE CONSTABLE: Well it could be at time of war.

BELL-BELL: We've been having a bazaar and rummage.

WOMAN POLICE CONSTABLE: Oh, is that what the smell is? I couldn't place it.

MARGARET: It's old clothes.

WOMAN POLICE CONSTABLE: Is everything all right then?

FLISS: Yes, we're going soon.

WOMAN POLICE CONSTABLE: Could I stay for a moment?

The WOMAN POLICE CONSTABLE *slumps.*

FLISS: Aren't you well?

BELL-BELL: Would you like a drink of water?

WOMAN POLICE CONSTABLE: No thank you, I've just had a cup of tea at the station.

There is a long, uncomfortable pause.

MARGARET (*breaking it*): Have you got the time?

WOMAN POLICE CONSTABLE: It's five fifty-seven and thirteen seconds, Madam. (*She is near to tears.*) It's a long while since anybody asked me the time.

FLISS: Do you mind if we get on?

WOMAN POLICE CONSTABLE: No, don't let me interfere in the course of your duties. I know how annoying that can be.

The WOMAN POLICE CONSTABLE *sits down heavily. The* WOMEN *start to pack away, looking every now and then at the* WOMAN POLICE CONSTABLE *who sits slumped in the chair. There are loud whispers, the* WOMAN POLICE CONSTABLE *is an intruder.*

MARGARET (*to* FLISS): What are we going to do with all this bleedin' rummage?

The trestle tables and chairs are put away.

KATRINA: Shush, Margaret! You'll get us done for obscene language. (*She looks at the* WOMAN POLICE CONSTABLE.)

FLISS: We're taking it with us.

MARGARET: Where are we going?

FLISS: Out!

The WOMAN POLICE CONSTABLE *sits with her head in her hands.*

BELL-BELL: What's wrong with her?

They all look at the WOMAN POLICE CONSTABLE.

MARGARET: I ain't seen her before, I thought I knew 'em all round here. Our Darren brings 'em home with him.

KATRINA *nervously approaches the* WOMAN POLICE CONSTABLE.

KATRINA (*smiles*): Excuse me. (*She is trying to charm the* WOMAN POLICE CONSTABLE.)

WOMAN POLICE CONSTABLE (*jerking*): Yes, Madam?

KATRINA: Could you give me a lift home please? I'm an agoraphobic.

WOMAN POLICE CONSTABLE: Frightened of cupboards are you?

KATRINA: No. The public. I was once pelted with plastic pineapples during my big finale.

MARGARET: Is that what they did to you, Kat?

KATRINA: Yes, one hit me in the eye. I had an awful bruise.

MARGARET: The bastards!

WOMAN POLICE CONSTABLE: I agree with you, Madam, the public are bastards, lying, thieving, undisciplined bastards.

FLISS: Are you sure you're in the right job?

WOMAN POLICE CONSTABLE: I was all right in my panda car, but they took it off me for sleeping on the hard shoulder. I was thrown on to the streets — community policing. But I only clocked on at five. (*She cries.*)

MARGARET: If she's scared, there's no bleedin' hope for us, is there?

KATRINA: The public can be terrible once they turn.

FLISS: But we're the public aren't we? For Christ's sake we're half the population. Why should we be forced to stay at bloody home? Come on, we're going out. Grab a bag and a box each.

KATRINA: I can't, Fliss.

BELL-BELL: Hold on to me, Katrina.

MARGARET: I'm shit scared, Fliss.

FLISS: We'll keep together. We'll be all right if we keep together.

WOMAN POLICE CONSTABLE: I joined because I wanted to help.

MARGARET: Come on then, Mrs Dixon, grab hold of this. (*She gives her a basket of shoes, then puts a box of toys and bric-à-brac on top.*) You look like a big, strong girl. Here!

BELL-BELL: You all right, Kat?

KATRINA: Yes. (*She laughs.*)

FLISS: Walk them down the path. Go
on. (*She shuts the piano lid with a
bang The* WOMAN POLICE
CONSTABLE *grabs the water pistol.*)
You won't be needing that. Go on!

The WOMAN POLICE CONSTABLE
crosses to the WOMEN *at the door.
They take a deep breath. They are
still terrified of the outside world.
They are not cured of their
agoraphobia. They are leaving because
they have no other choice.
The* WOMEN *move together in an
untidy, chaotic group holding bags and
boxes. They turn and look into the
hall. Then they leave.* KATRINA
*closes her eyes against the darkness
outside.* FLISS *picks up a bag and
box, looks around the room, crosses
to the crucifix and looks at it for a
moment.*

Cheer up!

*She crosses to the door, puts the lights
out, goes out and slams it shut.*

Blackout.

GROPING FOR WORDS

Groping for Words was first presented at the Croydon Warehouse Theatre on 10 March 1983, with the following cast:

KEVIN	Andrew Paul
JOYCE	Jan Davies
THELMA	Sarah Kenyon
GEORGE	Denys Graham

Directed by Sue Pomeroy
Designed by Kate Burnett
Sound by Carl Sutton
Lighting by Wiard Sterk

ACT ONE

Scene One

A small classroom in a Victorian school is furnished with tiny chairs and tables, a square of carpet, floor cushions, the usual crèche teaching aids: beans in jars, a goldfish nature table, blackboard, wendy house, bricks, little library and jars of paint. On the walls are real children's paintings, (3 to 5 years old). There is one door and a large stock cupboard facing the audience.
Voices are heard and keys rattle at the door. The door opens. KEVIN, *the caretaker, opens the door with some ceremony. He switches on the lights. He is wearing a short brown caretaker's coat, badges decorate the lapels. Underneath he wears a baggy 'Damned' T-shirt, blue jeans, big studded belt and training shoes. A copy of the* Sun *newspaper is sticking out of one pocket, a plastic container of darts is in his top pocket. His hair is slicked back 1950s American style. He is wearing one long dangling earring. His right hand is bandaged.*

KEVIN (*as he puts the lights on*): Here we go.

> JOYCE *enters the room. She is middle-class, expensively and conventionally dressed, and is carrying an 'organiser' handbag.*

KEVIN (*indicates the room*): This do you?

JOYCE: What is it?

KEVIN: It's the crèche.

JOYCE: So why are you showing it to me?

KEVIN: It's your room.

JOYCE: I'm teaching adults and I expect them to be the usual average height. (*She picks up a tiny chair with one finger.*) Could I see a proper classroom please?

She turns to leave.

KEVIN: There ain't one.

JOYCE: There is one. I booked it. I spoke to the caretaker last week.

KEVIN: Who, Horace?

JOYCE: A Mr Fillingham.

KEVIN: Bloke with a cleft palate?

JOYCE: He did sound rather indistinct over the phone.

KEVIN: Yeah, that's Horace. The Head Caretaker.

JOYCE: Where is he?

KEVIN: At home takin' care of himself for a change.

JOYCE: Why isn't he here doing his job? It's the first night of term.

KEVIN: He's been suspended for nickin' the cleanin' stuff.

JOYCE: So who's in charge?

KEVIN: Me. I'm Acting Head Caretaker until Horace has his court martial. He's bound to get done though. County Hall did a dawn swoop on his house. His box room was choc-a-block wiv dusters and bottles of bleach. (*Pause.*) His bleedin' house is filthy an' all.

JOYCE: I haven't time to listen to sordid little anecdotes, would you please show me to an adult-size classroom?

KEVIN: I keep tellin' you, there ain't one left. 'Livin' Wiv the Bomb' had the last one.

JOYCE: But there must be a room somewhere, this place is Victorian. The Victorians were extremely generous when it came to rooms.

KEVIN: An' it's full of people improving themselves. We've had a run on rooms. Look I'll have to go, I've got things to do.

> JOYCE *closes the door and stands in front of it.*

JOYCE: Oh no you don't, my lad.

KEVIN: Look the only empty room I've got is the boiler house an' it gets a bit hot in there.

JOYCE: Where's your allocations book?

KEVIN: I ain't got one, I carry it in me head.

JOYCE: Huh! That explains a great deal.

KEVIN: Whatja mean?

JOYCE: Well your outside appearance is extremely unprepossessing isn't it? I shudder to think what the *inside* of your head is like.

KEVIN: Let me out, I've got a ballcock to fix.

JOYCE: Not until you've given me your name and works number.

JOYCE takes a pad and pencil from her bag.

KEVIN: What for?

JOYCE: Reference.

KEVIN: Can't. (*He holds up his bandaged hand.*) I'm an injured soldier. (*Pause.*) A ferret took a bit out of my wrist.

JOYCE: In Clapham?

KEVIN: Straight up! I was cleaning its stinking cage out an' all. Ungrateful little bleeder! You do a dumb animal a good turn and where does it get you?

JOYCE: What's your name?

KEVIN: Kevin Muldoon.

JOYCE (*writes*): And your works number?

KEVIN: Well Horace is number one in the hierarchy so I must be number two.

JOYCE writes.
KEVIN is rebandaging his wrist.

JOYCE: You're making an awful mess of doing that. (*Pause.*) Have you had it looked at?

KEVIN: I look at it now an' again. It's alright apart from the gangrene.

JOYCE: Gangrene?

KEVIN (*laughs*): I wouldn't mind losing the odd finger, less weight to carry round ain't it?

JOYCE: I don't suppose you had a tetanus jab did you?

KEVIN: No I didn't. I'd sooner die of tetanus than have a needle stuck up me bum.

JOYCE: You're a very silly boy. And you're extremely lucky that you didn't get lockjaw. I have some medical knowledge and I've seen the consequences of neglect.

She is by now bandaging his wrist.

KEVIN (*admiringly*): The consequences of neglect – (*Pause.*) You weren't here last term were you?

JOYCE: No, tonight's my first night.

KEVIN: Oh, you ain't 'Coming to Terms With Death' are you?

JOYCE: No I'm not. I hardly give it a thought.

KEVIN: Good job. Right miserable sods've registered for that. All got one foot in the grave.

JOYCE: You really are a mess aren't you? You should take a pride in your appearance.

KEVIN: So should you.

JOYCE: Don't be so rude! I do. I'm neat and tidy.

KEVIN: Bit boring though. If you hadn't spoke, I wouldn't have noticed you. An' I was looking your way.

JOYCE: Yes, well. Unlike you I don't wish to thrust myself into the fore-ground. I'm quite happy melting into the distance.

JOYCE touches KEVIN's earring.

JOYCE: I'll never get used to seeing men wearing earrings. In my day one was suspicious of any man wearing suede shoes. Boys would follow them in the street, shouting 'Hello Oscar'.

KEVIN: Oscar who?

JOYCE: Oscar Wilde.

KEVIN: Who's he?

JOYCE: He's a very famous writer! He's a household name!

KEVIN: Not in our house he ain't.

JOYCE *completes pinning the bandage.*

KEVIN (*starts to remove his earring*): Wanna try it on?

JOYCE: No thank you. I can't wear cheap jewellery.

KEVIN: It ain't cheap! I paid two quid for this. Me mate makes 'em out of melted down bean tins. You pay for the labour, see. Go on, try it on.

JOYCE: Don't be so silly. My students will be arriving soon.

KEVIN: What you teachin'?

JOYCE: Literacy.

KEVIN: Books an' stuff? Well you'll be alright in here then, won't you? You can read books anywhere. My Grandma used to sit on the toilet to read her *Woman's Realm.*

JOYCE: You're mixing books up with magazines.

KEVIN: It's all writin' in it?

JOYCE *sighs and looks despondent.*

KEVIN: Tell you what. I'll swap you and the Buddhists over next week. They ain't into furniture.

JOYCE: Thank you.

KEVIN: Try it on. I wanna see what it looks like on you. I'm thinking of buying a pair for my auntie.

JOYCE *inclines her head, KEVIN brushes her hair away from her neck and ears.*

KEVIN: You got a nice neck for your age.

JOYCE: Thank you.

KEVIN: It's lovely an' soft. Clean an' all.

JOYCE *stiffens.*

KEVIN (*starts to insert earring*): You had a bath before you come out didn't you?

JOYCE (*weakly*): Yes.

KEVIN: You got a big gob of talcum here. Shall I rub it in for you?

JOYCE: No don't bother.

KEVIN: S'all right.

KEVIN *rubs the back of her neck.*

KEVIN: Lovely smell. Expensive I bet.

JOYCE: Sainsbury's, 76 pence family size.

KEVIN *adjusts her collar, pushes her hair behind her ears and gives the earring a final tweak.*

KEVIN: You deserve better than that. (*Pause.*) It takes ten years off you. You look (*Pause.*) forty-five.

JOYCE: I *am* forty-five.

KEVIN: All right thirty-five then. You gonna let me go now?

Pause, he smiles.

JOYCE: Yes, all right. If anybody enquires for Adult Literacy could you let them know that that's me and where I am?

KEVIN: Can't you just stick a notice up?

JOYCE: No, my students can't read. That's why they're coming.

KEVIN (*shocked*): Oh that's Literacy! (*Recovers.*) Poor sods, hard to credit it in this day an' age ain't it?

JOYCE: Yes it's very sad so please, be polite to them. They'll be awfully nervous.

KEVIN: It's the age we're livin' in, ain't it?

KEVIN *exits.*

JOYCE *takes a deep breath. She takes paper, pens, pencils and red exercise books out of her bag and arranges them on a little table. She takes her coat off, takes a mirror out of her bag and combs her hair.*

She looks at earring, grimaces, tries to take it out and can't do it. She struggles. She looks at her watch, struggles again and panics.
She takes her scarf out of her bag and ties it turban-like around her head and ears. She tucks the earring inside and looks in her hand mirror.

JOYCE: My God! It's Hilda Ogden! And I so wanted it to be Germaine Greer tonight. Stupid cow!

Scene Two

The corridor and caretakers' office and store.
A notice board listing the courses is on one wall. There is a sign saying 'lavatories'. KEVIN *is in his cubby hole, brooding over a box of papers and smoking a cigarette.* GEORGE *enters hesitantly, he is wearing an old suit, shirt and tie and carrying a cloth bag and a plastic Marks and Spencer carrier bag. His shoes are polished, he seems to have spent some time in a cubicle in a men's hostel trying to disguise his poverty. He has a red, blue and black pen in his jacket pocket.*

GEORGE: Evenin'.

KEVIN: Evenin'.

GEORGE: It's cold out there. *(He rubs his hands together.)*

KEVIN: It's winter. It's bound to be cold.

GEORGE: But we've not done bad have we, considering?

KEVIN: Look, I 'ate talkin' about the bleedin' weather.

GEORGE: Yes, it is somewhat restricted as a topic of conversation. There's not a lot you can say about it really is there? Rainy, hot, cold, misty, windy . . .

KEVIN *(more to himself)*: Barmy!

GEORGE: Yes, balmy. *(Pause.)* And humid's not a bad word.

KEVIN: Do you mind, only I'm doin' me paperwork. *(He rattles the box.)*

GEORGE: Sorry. *(Pause.)* Do you mind if I have a peruse?

KEVIN: Feel free, peruse away. *(He raises his eyes.)*

GEORGE *peers at the notice board,* KEVIN *reads.*

KEVIN: Are you for 'Comin' to Terms With Death'?

GEORGE: No, I'm only fifty-seven! *(Pause.)* I don't know what I'm here for. I'm a bit undecided. I can't quite make up me mind.

KEVIN: You sound like a natural for 'Positive Thinking', pity the tutor rang and cancelled.

GEORGE: What else is there?

KEVIN: It's all up there. *(He points to notice board.)* 'Creative Wine Drinkin's full though. Had to turn 'em away. It ain't everyday you can get pissed on the rates though, is it?

GEORGE: You ought to take the notice down then. Folks'll be disappointed. I don't mind for myself. I'm a beer man, wine's not my cup of tea.

KEVIN *comes out of his cubby hole.*

KEVIN: I'm into cocktails. Quite heavily into 'em.

GEORGE: Bit expensive in't it, for a young lad like you?

KEVIN: I can afford it. I'm in full-time employment. I'm one of the few. I work so that three and a half million can be free.

GEORGE: That's one way of looking at it.

KEVIN: It's the only way. Survival of the fittest in this world ain't it? Which one *says* 'Creative Wine Drinkin'? I've come out without me glasses.

GEORGE: Sorry I can't help you there.

I've got new contact lenses in and me eyes are swimmin'.

KEVIN (*staring into* GEORGE'*s eyes*): I can't see no contact lenses.

GEORGE: No, but then you wouldn't would you? Not if you've not got your glasses.

Awkward pause.

KEVIN: There's 'Know Your Engine'.

He points randomly at the notice. board.

You got a car?

GEORGE: No, I'm a pedestrian. I prefer walking.

KEVIN: Gettaway! You're the first *I've* met!

Pause.

KEVIN (*impatiently*): Well have a look at the notice and choose yourself something! I've got these forms to fill in.

GEORGE *moves off, then turns.*

GEORGE: Is there ought about writing up there?

KEVIN: 'Creative Writing's down the corridor. Bit of a Shakespeare are you?

GEORGE: Not so you'd notice.

Telephone rings inside cubicle.

KEVIN (*answers phone*): 'ello, Kevin Muldoon, Head Caretaker 'ere.

Tiny pause.

Spoggy! How ya doin'?

Pause.

Fuck me, we only done one last night!

Pause.

Yeah all right. What's the address?

He sees GEORGE *listening and half shuts his door.*

GEORGE *takes an airmail envelope from out of his inside jacket pocket. He takes a letter out and looks at it. He moons over a photograph and kisses it.*

THELMA *enters.*

GEORGE *puts the letter back in his pocket and stares at* THELMA. THELMA *is wearing dance class gear underneath very unmodish winter clothing. She is a young twenty year old. She should convey a bizarre appearance.*

THELMA: I'm looking for the lavatory, do you know where it is? The Ladies' lavatory, that is?

GEORGE: No, I've had no call to know, being a man.

THELMA: I shall *have* to find it.

She does a little cross-legged dance. GEORGE *looks anxiously up and down the corridor.*

GEORGE: The Caretaker's in there, but he's on the telephone.

THELMA *bangs on the cubicle door.* KEVIN *opens the door angrily.*

KEVIN: I'm on the phone. (He *speaks into phone*.) Hang on, Spoggy.

THELMA: Where's the Ladies' lavatory?

KEVIN (*to* THELMA): Hang on!

THELMA: I can't hang on! (*She is near to tears.*)

KEVIN (*into phone*): Right, I'll have to go. See you about half-past eleven at your place then.

Short pause.

(*Into phone*): Right. See you. (*He puts the phone down.*)

THELMA (*to* GEORGE): It's because I'm nervous. I know it's all in my head but . . .

KEVIN *comes out of the cubicle.*

KEVIN: Yeah, well keep it there. I only done this floor an hour ago. Down that corridor, second on the left.

THELMA *checks her left and right, then rushes off leaving her tote bag on the floor.*

KEVIN (*indicating lavatory sign*): I dunno, you go to the trouble to make bleedin' signs out, but do people bother to read em? Do they buggery!

GEORGE: She's left her bag.

KEVIN: She'll be back for it. You know what women are like about their bleedin' handbags. (*He picks the bag up and puts it in the cubicle.*)

GEORGE (*plucking up his courage*): Have you got ought like a reading room here?

KEVIN: Yeah. But it has to be locked up at night. Some of these self-improvers are right tea leaves. Mind you half the bleedin' books are collectors' items. Been here since the building was opened.

KEVIN *brings his tool box.*

GEORGE: Can you manage with that hand?

KEVIN: Yeah, I got used to the pain, in fact I think it's made me a better 'uman bein'.

GEORGE: How did you do it?

KEVIN: I slipped and fell on a cocktail stick. Went in one side. (*He holds his bandaged hand up.*) And came out the other. I 'ad to go down casualty and have the cherry removed.

GEORGE *walks back to look at the notice board.*

GEORGE (*quietly to himself*): Silly bugger!

THELMA *rushes in anxiously.*

THELMA: Where's my bag?

KEVIN: It's in 'ere. Keep your hair on. (*He picks up the bag.*)

THELMA: You shouldn't touch other people's property! Especially mine!

KEVIN: Why? What you got in here? A bomb? Dirty books? It's heavy ain't it? Let's 'ave a look!

He unzips the bag.

THELMA (*shrieks*): Don't! (*She snatches the bag from* KEVIN.)

KEVIN: All right! All right! Keep the noise down. You'll disturb the Buddhists.

THELMA: I'd like to report that there's a man in the Ladies' toilet. He's in the last cubicle.

KEVIN: How do you know?

THELMA: Because I could see his feet underneath the door.

KEVIN: Yeah, well the Ladies is bisexual tonight on account of flooding trouble in the Gents.

THELMA: You might have warned me. I wasn't prepared for it.

KEVIN: There's a notice on the door ain't there?

THELMA: No. There's a piece of toilet paper with rude drawings of a lady and a man.

KEVIN: They ain't rude! They're international symbols. Even an Eskimo would understand what they meant.

THELMA: Well I'm not an Eskimo, am I?

KEVIN *scrutinises* THELMA.

KEVIN: Dunno, you could be, it's hard to tell what you are under all that gear.

THELMA: I'm Miss Thelma Churchill. *(Automatically,)* no relation. I registered over the phone. I don't trust the post.

KEVIN: It weren't me you spoke to.

THELMA: Well whoever it was he said he'd put my name in the book.

KEVIN: What book?

THELMA: I don't know! I was on the other end of the phone wasn't I? I was in Kensington.

Pause. KEVIN *is sorting through papers in a box.*

THELMA: And there's no toilet paper

in the toilet either. (*Pause*.)
You ought to have a system.

KEVIN *waves a piece of paper about.*

KEVIN: Here it is. Miss Thelma Churchill. Room eleven and you'd better hurry, they're about to break the pain barrier.

THELMA *fiddles around in her bag.*

KEVIN: Right, I'm off on an errand of mercy. (*He picks up a double pack of toilet paper.*) Before they start wiping their bums on *The Standard* and clogging my 'S' bends.

KEVIN *exits.*

THELMA: Are you in a position of authority?

GEORGE: No I'm just looking.

THELMA: Oh. I thought you might be a teacher.

GEORGE (*pleased*): Did you? I expect it's because I'm wearing a tie, there's not many bother now-a-days.

THELMA: No it's the pens, I like to see a pen in a man's pocket. It imparts an air of learning. My father had a very impressive array.

They stare at each other, then drop eye contact and shuffle.

THELMA: Do you know where room eleven is?

GEORGE: No. I'm a stranger here myself.

THELMA *looks around anxiously.*

GEORGE (*indicating notice board*): Can you see ought up there about reading and writing? I've come out without me glasses.

THELMA: It's no good asking me. I've got a disease, it stops me reading properly.

GEORGE: Oh I *am* sorry, is it painful?

THELMA: No it's nothing like that. It's a brain problem.

GEORGE: Oh dear. Are you under the hospital?

THELMA (*contemptuously*): Them! They don't know what they're on about, do they? It's a waste of time going down there. My mother took me to a private brain consultant. She said, 'My Thelma's got dyslexia.' He said, 'Who says?' My mum said, 'I say.' She'd been reading up on it, but he wouldn't have it! He wouldn't listen! He said that I was over-anxious! And he tried to give me and my mother something for our nerves! We were that disgusted we walked out! We thought about reporting him, but what's the point? They all stick up for each other don't they?

GEORGE: Yes they're bound by their hypocritical oath.

THELMA: Do you know what time it is? I've got to register at half-past seven.

GEORGE (*bringing out alarm clock*): It's a quarter to eight! I'm late. Me first lesson and I'm late! (*He panics and stuffs his gear into his bag.*)

THELMA: A quarter to eight! Oh no! I shall be told off!

JOYCE *enters, still wearing the scarf. She goes to the cubicle and sees* KEVIN *isn't there.*

JOYCE (*to* THELMA): Excuse me. Have you seen the caretaker?

THELMA: The scruffy one?

JOYCE: Yes.

THELMA: Sorry, you're not his mother are you?

JOYCE: Certainly not!

GEORGE: He's gone off replenishing supplies.

JOYCE: Oh dear . . . (*to* THELMA:) Look, I know this is perfectly absurd, but could you help me with this wretched earring? (*She has taken her scarf off.*) I can't get it out on my own. I've been struggling for . . . (*She gives a feeble laugh.*)

THELMA: I've never seen one like that before. I wouldn't know where to begin. And anyway I'm supposed to be in my night-class, do you know where room eleven is?

JOYCE: Upstairs, next to the big hall.

THELMA *rushes off.*

GEORGE: Do you want me to have a go?

JOYCE: It's very kind of you . . . but I don't want to detain you. You look as if you're on your way somewhere.

GEORGE: No. No. I'm just . . . here.

JOYCE: Well perhaps we could go into my room. This is very embarrassing. I wouldn't wear anything like this normally . . .

GEORGE *is peering at the earring.*

GEORGE: You just fancied a change did you? Well why not?

JOYCE: But I'm expecting students and first impressions are so important aren't they?

GEORGE: Yes. They colour everything. Once seen never forgotten . . . Well if you'll just sort of bend your head.

JOYCE *bends*, GEORGE *twists and turns trying to avoid body contact while he unfastens the earring.*

Scene Three

In the créche.

GEORGE: You're an infant teacher are you? (*He puts his bags down.*)

JOYCE: No, I teach adults. At least I'm hoping to, nobody seems to have turned up yet.

GEORGE: If you could sit down sort of . . .

JOYCE *sits on a little chair.* GEORGE *squats at her side.*

GEORGE: I don't know how to tackle it. It's in a right old mess.

JOYCE: If I put my head to one side like this . . . (*She turns her head away from* GEORGE.)

GEORGE: That's better. Now the dog can see the rabbit.

Scene Four

Back outside KEVIN*'s cubicle.* THELMA *is waiting.* KEVIN *enters.*

THELMA: You sent me to the wrong place! I don't want to go to Jane Fonda's robotics classes.

KEVIN: How did I know? You look like a robot. You're dressed like a robot. You even sound like one.

THELMA: Well I'm not. I put my name down for the reading lessons. It's in the book.

KEVIN: What readin'? We got Shakespeare Can Be Fun . . . Clapham Playwrights' Circle . . .

THELMA: This is *just* reading. From the beginning, starting from scratch.

KEVIN: Literacy is the word you're looking for.

THELMA: No it isn't! I don't know what it means so how can I be looking for it?

KEVIN: Adult Literacy. Room six.

THELMA: Where's that?

KEVIN: Bleedin' 'ell! It's up there in black and white! Can't you do numbers either?

THELMA: No, not when I'm upset.

KEVIN: Come on!

They leave for JOYCE*'s room.*

Scene Five

JOYCE*'s room.*

JOYCE (*loud scream*): Ah! That hurt!

GEORGE: I'm sorry. Shall I desist?

JOYCE: No just get it out will you?

GEORGE: Just one more pull. (*He tugs.*)

JOYCE *screams.*

GEORGE: Shall I proceed?

JOYCE: Yes I'm sorry, it's just that I've got a very low pain threshold.

GEORGE: I don't like hurting you.

JOYCE: No please go on, hurt me.

GEORGE: Right. One, two, three ready?

JOYCE *nods,* GEORGE *tugs,* JOYCE *screams louder and falls over,* GEORGE *falls on top of her.* KEVIN *runs in, jumps astride* GEORGE's *chest and pins his arms down.* THELMA *enters.*

KEVIN: You dirty bleeder!

(*He turns to* THELMA): Ring 999 and tell 'em I've got the Wandsworth Wanker.

THELMA *moves towards the door.*

JOYCE: Don't you dare!

KEVIN (*to* JOYCE): He didn't touch you did he?

KEVIN *threatens* GEORGE *with a head butt.*

THELMA: I thought he had funny eyes!

THELMA *is helping* JOYCE *up.*

KEVIN: Yes I had him marked down as a deviant, they all wear pens in their top pockets. It's a well-know fact that is.

JOYCE (*to* KEVIN): Get off him! Get off! You're hurting him.

JOYCE (*to* GEORGE): I'm terribly sorry.

THELMA: Shall I fetch the police?

KEVIN: Yeah.

JOYCE (*shouting to* KEVIN): Get off! Get off!

(*She pushes* KEVIN, *then turns to* GEORGE.) Are you all right?

GEORGE: No, I'm having a few difficulties breathing.

THELMA: What is it, 999?

KEVIN: Yeah, go on! Just wait 'til

they get you down the nick, pervert. They'll knock the breath out of you permanent. You'll be lucky if you come out there with your balls intact.

THELMA: They ought to castrate them.

KEVIN (*to* THELMA): What you waiting for?

THELMA: Have you got five p?

JOYCE *is pushing* KEVIN, *she is grunting with the effort.*

GEORGE (*to* KEVIN): I was very careful to avoid any erotic contact. I kept strictly away from any danger zones.

KEVIN: Not far enough! She's a decent woman. She's got Marks and Spencer labels all over her!

JOYCE (*bellows*): Leave him alone! He was doing me a favour!

She punches KEVIN *repeatedly.*

THELMA: I shall have to go. All this violence is unsettling me.

JOYCE (*to* GEORGE): Don't just lie there man! Help me!

GEORGE *wrestles* KEVIN *backwards.* KEVIN *lies on the floor panting.*

GEORGE: That's the last time I help a stranger out of a dilemma situation.

JOYCE *and* GEORGE *kneel together, mutually supporting each other, dishevelled and breathing heavily.*

JOYCE (*to* GEORGE): I'm awfully sorry.

(*to* KEVIN): This gentleman was removing your odious earring. You owe him a grovelling apology.

THELMA (*to* KEVIN): You must have a mind like a sewer, in fact a cess pit.

KEVIN: I thought he was the Wandsworth Wanker. I have to be careful, you get a lot of nutters coming to night classes. They've got the time for it.

GEORGE: It was a case of mistaken identify was it? (*Worried.*) Do I look like this Wandsworth . . . (*Gags at saying wanker*) . . . ladies present.

KEVIN: Nobody's seen his face, he wears a pair of 'Y' fronts over his head. So you could have been him see?

GEORGE: Yes I quite understand. Here. (*He hands* KEVIN *the earring.*)

GEORGE: It's a funny shape for an earring.

JOYCE: Yes, it's made out of a baked bean tin.

THELMA: Crosse and Blackwell or Heinz?

KEVIN: It's symbolic.

JOYCE: Of what?

KEVIN: Society and how it screws you up. (*He offers it to* JOYCE.) Do you wanna keep it?

JOYCE: No thank you. I don't wish to be regarded as one of society's victims.

GEORGE (*dusting himself off*): Well I'd better depart. (*He starts repacking his belongings.*)

KEVIN (*indicates* THELMA): I found you a student.

JOYCE: Oh, I'll be with you in a moment, dear. Hello.

THELMA: Hello.

KEVIN: Anybody else turned up yet?

JOYCE: No, not yet.

KEVIN: You should try teaching something a bit more popular. Cocktail Shakin', somethin' like that. Adult Literacy! Don't reach out and grab you, do it?

GEORGE: You teach Adult Literacy do you? That must be very interesting.

JOYCE: Yes. I'm sure it is. Perhaps one day I'll find out.

KEVIN: Can't imagine not readin' or writin' can you?

JOYCE: You'll be surprised how many there are.

GEORGE: Two million they reckon. It was on Radio Four. Jill Archer told Walter Gabriel.

THELMA: Your ear's bleeding. Do you want a plaster on it?

JOYCE: Yes please. My husband warned me about coming into Clapham at night, he said I'd return home blood-stained. I'd hate to give him the satisfaction of being right.

THELMA: There's a washbasin in the bisexual lavatory. I've got some cotton wool in my bag, I could see to it for you. I know what I'm doing, I was in the St. John's Ambulance once.

JOYCE: Thank you.

JOYCE *and* THELMA *exit.*

GEORGE: So she's the teacher is she? I didn't expect a woman somehow.

KEVIN: You don't want to go to her class. You heard her, she's for the dumbo's what can't read.

GEORGE: All the same I think I'll have a word with her. I've got a friend who's a bit rusty on his reading. She might be able to help him.

GEORGE *sits down.*

KEVIN: Hey! How's Joe Grundy doing? I ain't heard it since me Grandma died.

GEORGE (*pleased*): He's cheered up a lot since Clarrie's happy event.

KEVIN: Eddie still giving him bovver is he?

GEORGE: Yes, that's one lad who'll never change.

KEVIN: It's hard to change yourself though, ain't it? Least, that's what I've found.

GEORGE: It's making the first move that's the hardest.

KEVIN: See you around. Sorry about the bit of bovver.

GEORGE: Oh I'm getting used to it now I'm domiciled in London. It's part of my daily existence.

KEVIN *exits.* GEORGE *picks up the text books, looks through them, decides that the contents are beyond him and loses his nerve. He picks up his belongings and exits into the corridor.*

Scene Six

The corridor and KEVIN*'s cubby hole. Follow on from last scene.* GEORGE *passes* KEVIN *who is throwing darts savagely into the notice board.*

KEVIN: You ain't staying for a chat then?

GEORGE: What?

KEVIN: About your friend's reading?

GEORGE: No. He's decided not to bother.

KEVIN: You're in telepathic communication are you?

GEORGE: No, he's not on the phone.

GEORGE *exits.*

Scene Seven

In the classroom. Follow on from last scene. THELMA *and* JOYCE *enter.* JOYCE *is holding a piece of cotton wool to her ear.*

THELMA (*gushing*): It's a lovely little room isn't it? I didn't have time to notice it before, and you've even got a goldfish! He's got a lovely little face.

Pause.

(*She turns to the fish*): What's your name then?

JOYCE: Joyce Chalmers.

THELMA: That's a funny name for a fish.

JOYCE: The fish's name is written on the bowl.

THELMA *turns her back on* JOYCE.

THELMA (*in a totally different grown-up voice*): I've just told you I can't read, so it's no good telling me that is it?

JOYCE (*crossing to the bowl*): I'm sorry. It says 'DARREN'.

THELMA: Darren? How do they know it's a boy? Hello Darren. I love all living creatures, don't you?

JOYCE: Not quite all.

JOYCE *finds a plaster and a pair of children's blunt scissors, she gives them to* THELMA.

JOYCE: Would you mind? Then we can get down to some work can't we?

THELMA: Oh aren't they sweet! Just think about all the chubby little fingers that have held these scissors.

JOYCE *sits down on a tiny chair,* THELMA *stands over her. She pulls* JOYCE*'s head around and prepares to place the plaster.*

THELMA: I shall have to take my things off first. I can't move my arms.

She removes her scarf and coat and leaves her hat on. She is now looking distinctly odd. She is wearing a neon body stocking, leg warmers, a P.E. skirt, granny boots and a hideous shrunken cardigan which says 'Thelma' on the back. Her cardigan has a 'T' brooch hanging loosely from it. She is also wearing a chain necklace with a 'T' pendant.

THELMA: I promised Mum that I'd wrap up warm when I came down to London. I've got a chest – and bad ears.

JOYCE: Have you lived in London long?

THELMA: No. I've only been here for three weeks. But I know it really well already.

JOYCE: I hardly know it at all and I've lived here all my life.

THELMA: You ought to go on a double-decker tour of the tourist spots. It's the only way to see it properly. It gets a bit blowy so make sure you wear something over your ears.

THELMA *puts the plaster on.*

There!

JOYCE: Thank you. Right, now if you'll give me a moment to get myself sorted out.

THELMA: You're going grey, did you know?

JOYCE (*with gritted teeth*): I've known for some years.

THELMA: I only pointed it out in case you wanted to do something about it.

There is a knock on the door.

JOYCE: Excuse me.

She opens the door, GEORGE *is standing there.*

GEORGE: Sorry for disturbing the peace. I'm Mr Bishop. I know we've been in contact, but we haven't met.

They shake hands solemnly.

JOYCE: Come in. (*She ushers him in:*) I'm Mrs Chalmers. Joyce.

GEORGE: Can I have a word with you? Well more than one to be exact. A few words. (*He sees* THELMA *and drops his head.*) In private so to speak.

He wipes his face with his hands.

JOYCE (*to* THELMA): I don't know your name do I?

THELMA: Thelma Churchull, no relation.

JOYCE: Thelma would you mind if I spoke to Mr Bishop privately? Alone?

THELMA: Do you mean you want me to go into another room?

GEORGE: Sorry to put you out. Inconvenience you.

THELMA: I've only just got here myself!

THELMA *goes into the wendy house and sits down.* JOYCE *and* GEORGE *stand awkwardly looking at the wendy house.*

JOYCE (*in a loud whisper to* GEORGE): Is this private enough?

GEORGE (*to* THELMA): Would you mind closing the door?

THELMA *bangs the wendy house door shut and pulls the curtains. Pause.*

GEORGE: Well, it's took me a long while to get here and now I'm here I can't seem to . . . say what I came here to say.

JOYCE: Shall we sit down? (JOYCE *sits down on a tiny chair.*)

GEORGE: I'm used to standing, I'm a pedestrian. (*He remains standing.*)

JOYCE (*after a pause*): Is it connected with reading?

GEORGE: Yes.

JOYCE: And writing?

GEORGE: Yes. I've got a friend who's a bit rusty.

JOYCE: And your friend needs help with his reading and writing?

GEORGE: He can't read and he can't write. He's illiterate so to speak. But he's made up his mind to do something about it. He's getting on a bit. As a matter of fact he's the same age as me or thereabouts. Give or take a week. But he says he's had enough of guessin' and tellin' lies. He's fed up with it. He's had enough. He's not too old is he?

JOYCE: No.

Long pause.

JOYCE: When does your friend want to start?

GEORGE: As soon as possible.

JOYCE: Does he live in London?

GEORGE: Yes he's down here looking for work. He's not having much luck. There's a lot of avenues closed to him.

JOYCE: Shall I give you a few details?

GEORGE *sits down on a tiny chair.*

GEORGE: Details, yes that's what he wants.

JOYCE: We meet on Wednesdays from half seven to half nine. It will cost your friend fourteen pounds a term . . .

GEORGE: Oh, he thought it was free.

JOYCE: No, unfortunately we have to pay for the room.

GEORGE *looks round.*

JOYCE: We won't be in here every week. Don't worry. (*Pause.*) Tell your friend not to worry. (*Pause.*) Will the money be a problem to your friend?

GEORGE: He's out of work you see. He hasn't got fourteen pounds. Not on him.

Long pause.

JOYCE: You could pay me so much a week. Would that be convenient?

GEORGE: Yes. (*He lowers his head, ashamed of lying.*) When can I start?

JOYCE: Tonight.

GEORGE: Right, that's all right then. (*He smiles.*)

JOYCE: And your full name is?

GEORGE (*very drawn out*): George Arthur Bishop.

JOYCE *writes.*

JOYCE: And where are you living Mr Bishop?

GEORGE: In London.

JOYCE: Whereabouts?

GEORGE (*evasively*): Not far from here.

JOYCE: I have to register you with the Education Authority. So I'll need your full address.

GEORGE: Care of the Rowton Ho . . . Hotel, Wandsworth Road.

JOYCE: Can I reach you on the telephone there?

GEORGE: Oh no. I'm incommunicado in that respect. (*Slight pause.*) And

they're not too keen on their guests having visitors either, that's the rules.

JOYCE (*slight laugh*): It doesn't sound a very hospitable hotel. Who's it run by, the War Office?

GEORGE: It's sort of run on military lines.

JOYCE: Oh a sort of ex-serviceman's club! I see.

THELMA *draws the curtains and sticks her head out of the window.*

THELMA: Can I come out now? Only, the walls are closing in on me.

GEORGE *gets up and opens the door,* THELMA *shuffles out on her hands and knees.* GEORGE *helps her to her feet.*

THELMA: Are you learning as well?

GEORGE: Yes, why are you?

THELMA: I was here first. (*To* JOYCE:) Are you sure you can manage two? I saw a programme on telly and this man had a teacher to himself. He got on ever so well. He was reading the *Sun* within weeks.

JOYCE: The *Sun!* My dear girl we're going to set our sights a little higher than that.

GEORGE *sits down and wipes his face.*

JOYCE: Miss Churchill, Mr Bishop . . .

GEORGE: Very nice to . . . (*he stands up and the chair comes with him. They shake hands.*)

JOYCE: I'll need your address, Thelma.

THELMA: Do you want to know where I live now, or where I really live? Because I really live in Northampton. I'm only here in London because of my job. It takes too long to travel to Northampton every day. I don't know how those computers manage it, going backwards and forwards.

JOYCE: Your London address is fine.

THELMA: 10, Gladstone Mansions, Kensington.

JOYCE *writes it down.*

JOYCE: Why have you come all the way to Clapham?

THELMA: I don't want Mrs Eirenstone to find out. She thinks I can read.

JOYCE: Mrs Eirenstone is your employer, is she?

THELMA: Yes. I look after her children. She's one of those working mothers who couldn't do without me. And I don't want her to do without me. I love London. It's got a bit more life than Northampton. There's more to do at night.
Mrs Eirenstone's out every night, she's ever so popular. You should see her clothes! I've known her pay twenty pounds for a scarf! Hard to believe isn't it? But it's true. Twenty pounds!

GEORGE: She sounds a wonderful woman, a bit extravagant perhaps but vibrant. Is she having a night in tonight then?

THELMA: Yes. She's having a row with Mr Eirenstone. (*Pause.*) Mrs Eirenstone has asked me to teach Davina, that's her little girl, to read.

JOYCE: Oh I see.

THELMA: She's got her into a very expensive school, you see, and Davina will feel left out if she doesn't know how to read.

JOYCE: How old is Davina?

THELMA: She was three at Christmas. Mrs Eirenstone has sent away for the early reading books. In fact they've already come. But Mrs Eirenstone doesn't know yet.

GEORGE: You intercepted the postman did you?

THELMA: No, I took the parcel and shoved it in the back of my wardrobe. I have to take it out with me if I go out. I've been carrying it around all week. (*She pulls the parcel out of her bag and puts it on the table.*) So if you can teach me to read these I'd be ever so grateful.

JOYCE *thumbs through the early reading books.*

JOYCE (*disapprovingly*): But these books were written in the 1940s and they're far too simple.

THELMA: Well I'm simple myself. Least that's what they said at school. (*Little laugh.*) I was bottom of the class. 31 out of 31.

JOYCE: But Thelma, my approach is going to be quite different. These books are written for very small children. I'd like you to leave me in a few years being able to read everything.

THELMA: A few years! But I haven't got that long! Mrs Eirenstone's already talking about complaining to the Post Office about the late delivery.

GEORGE: I can't wait a few years either. I've got a daughter in Australia! It's not the reading I'm so bothered about, it's the writing. I want to learn to write so I can reply to her letters.

He pulls an air mail letter out of his pocket.

Look! (*He passes it to* JOYCE.) She's a lovely writer isn't she? She won a prize at school. She got *Uncle Tom's Cabin* for neatness of handwriting.

JOYCE: Yes. (*She hands it back.*) Very nice.

GEORGE: Would you like to see her photograph?

He passes a photograph.

JOYCE: What a pretty girl!

THELMA: Can I have a look? (*She looks.*) She's lovely looking isn't she? She's not a bit like you. What's that funny shape in the background?

GEORGE: That's her husband, Malcolm.

THELMA: No the *big* funny shape?

JOYCE *looks.*

JOYCE: It's the Sydney Opera House. My husband was there last year.

GEORGE: Has he got kith and kin in the antipodes?

JOYCE: No, he was there on holiday. He's a Grand Opera lover. At least he was until he saw the Sydney Opera House.

THELMA: And he didn't take you? That's not very fair is it?

JOYCE (*this still rankles*): No it wasn't, was it? I mentioned it to him at the time.

GEORGE (*gazing at photo*): She'd do anything for anybody. You could warm your hands on her heart. (*His face crumples.*)

JOYCE *stands and pats him on the back.*

JOYCE (*kindly*): It won't be long before you can reply. I'll help you, that's what I'm here for, isn't it?

GEORGE: But I can't even read it. I don't know how she is or ought.

JOYCE: But somebody would have read it to you.

GEORGE: Who?

JOYCE: Anybody.

GEORGE: I didn't just want *anybody* reading her letter.

JOYCE: Haven't you got a family?

GEORGE: In Australia. My wife, her new husband and my girl and her husband. They're all out there to grasp the opportunities. They're carving out better futures.

JOYCE: Friends at work?

GEORGE: I haven't got any work. Not anymore.

JOYCE: I see. Perhaps when you know me better . . . I'd be pleased to.

GEORGE: You can read it now! (*He holds the letter out.*)

JOYCE: But we really ought to get on. I need to find out what you can both do.

GEORGE: Can't do more like. (GEORGE *moons over the letter.*)

THELMA (*to* GEORGE): And I'm in a hurry. It's not fair on me if she starts reading your letters.

JOYCE (*to* GEORGE): How many pages are there?

GEORGE: Just the one.

JOYCE (*to* THELMA): Do you know what tracing is?

THELMA: Of course I do! I'm not that stupid! Honestly!

JOYCE: I have to ask, don't I?

THELMA: I know what most words *mean*. It's the writing and reading stage I'm stuck on.

JOYCE: Can you write your name?

THELMA: I can do Thelma.

JOYCE: But not your surname, not Churchill?

THELMA: No, I was away when we did surnames.

JOYCE: I'm going to write 'Churchill'. (*She writes Churchill in very large print on a flash card.*)

THELMA: That's too big! I'd never write it that big would I?

JOYCE: It's to get you used to the shape of the letters.

THELMA: It seems stupid to me! It's a waste of time.

JOYCE: Look, I know what I'm doing.

GEORGE: She's trained for years to be a teacher. Haven't you Mrs Chalmers?

JOYCE: Not years.

GEORGE: Well a year then.

JOYCE: Not a year, no.

GEORGE: Some months then?

JOYCE: Six weeks.

GEORGE: Six weeks is a long time (*Pause.*) Quite long.

THELMA: So you're not a proper teacher?

JOYCE: I'm trained to teach literacy.

THELMA: I thought I'd be in the hands of an expert. I need expert attention. I'm very slow.

JOYCE: Who said?

THELMA: The school. They said I was backward.

JOYCE: You're not backward, Thelma.

THELMA: Oh yes I am! Cleverer people than you have told me I am!

JOYCE: Mr Bishop, would you mind stepping out a moment?

GEORGE (*holding up the letter*): What about . . .

JOYCE: Two minutes.

GEORGE *exits into corridor.*

JOYCE: I'm going to tell you something, Thelma. (*Dramatic pause, her intention is to galvanise* THELMA.) I'm a very clever woman. I'm cleverer than any of your teachers at school. I could have been a professor of English if I'd wanted, but I thought it might be more fun to get married and live in Streatham, so I did, and it wasn't. (*Small pause.*) But! I carried on studying and reading and I got cleverer and cleverer. I wouldn't be surprised if I'm not some sort of genius by now, actually. Then I thought what shall I do with all this cleverness? (THELMA *is wrapped up in the story.*) I know! I said. I'll be a literacy tutor. I'll share my genius. So you see Thelma, just by coming into contact with me, *your* brain power is automatically increased. You *will* learn to read and write, because *I* Joyce Chalmers, am teaching you.

THELMA: Oh I see, that's a different complexion isn't it?

JOYCE: Yes, so trace over my letters will you?

THELMA *picks up a pencil.*

JOYCE: Hold the pencil a bit further down.

JOYCE *adjusts the pencil for* THELMA. THELMA *traces very carefully over the letters. Her tongue is out, she is tense and anxious.*

Scene Eight

GEORGE *is in the corridor talking to* KEVIN *in his cubicle.*

KEVIN: Your friend change his mind did he?

GEORGE: I thought I might as well ask for him as I was in the vicinity.

KEVIN: You been having a long chat, ain't you?

GEORGE: You know how it is, one word leads to another and before you know it you're having a conversation. (*Pause.*) Finding you've got things in common.

KEVIN: What have you and that dumbo teacher got in common then?

GEORGE (*pause*): Well we're both interested in . . . Rolf Harris.

KEVIN: Rolf Harris! What's interesting about Rolf Harris?

GEORGE: How he gets away with it, I suppose.

KEVIN: Here, do you reckon if I wobbled a bit of cardboard and threw a bit of paint on the wall, I'd end up living in a mansion with peacocks on the lawn?

GEORGE: He lives in a mansion does he?

KEVIN: Yes, with round-the-clock alsations.

GEORGE: How do you know?

KEVIN: I don't do I? I just make it up, it keeps me brain active. I might be needing it one day.

GEORGE: In what capacity?

KEVIN: Well I might go in for an education.

GEORGE: Yes, it's just as well to have something to fall back on.

KEVIN: Bloke I know murdered his next-door neighbour. Got ten years in Gartree, does six, comes out with a degree in English literature.

GEORGE: That's wonderful! (*Slight pause.*) Bit hard on the next-door neighbour though.

KEVIN: He should have turned his stereo down when he was asked.

GEORGE: Mind if I sit down? (*He sits on the floor.*)

KEVIN: No. You *look* knackered.

GEORGE: I am, I didn't get any sleep last night. We had a little unpleasantness at the . . . er . . . hotel. One of the guests went a little berserk and stabbed a social worker. It caused a bit of a rumpus. Fortunately the injuries were superficial.

KEVIN: Yeah, I heard about that, only it wasn't a hotel it was a hostel.

GEORGE: Yes, yes that's right a hostel. I keep getting it wrong.

KEVIN: Bleeding horrible place that is. You don't want to stay there, you'll catch something.

GEORGE: And the residents are quite troublesome. If they're not drunk they're stealing off you. I had an overcoat once.

KEVIN: So where are you kipping tonight then?

GEORGE: I don't know. Me Post Office book is down to seventeen pence. I'm in the hands of fate so to speak.

JOYCE (*off*): Mr Bishop.

GEORGE: I've got to go.

KEVIN: Yeah. Lucky you. She ain't bad for an old bird is she?

Scene Nine

GEORGE *enters the classroom.*

GEORGE: Miss Churchill looks busy. What are you doing?

THELMA: Don't! You'll make me go wrong.

JOYCE: Over here Mr Bishop, I'll read your letter.

They settle down.

JOYCE: 'Dear Dad, Well we got here after a safe journey. Malcolm didn't like the plane but I thought it was fantastic. I'm sitting writing to you in shorts and a halter neck on account of how hot it is here. Malcolm got sunburned and had to have the doctor. But he is all right now.

GEORGE: He's very fair skinned.

JOYCE (*reading*): 'Malcolm has gone to see his Auntie Kath, that's why I have a few moments to spare. Gordon . . .

GEORGE: Gordon's my wife's husband.

JOYCE (*reading*): is still getting on my nerves. I'll never take to him Dad. Still, me and Malcolm will soon have our own place with a bit of luck. We are still in the hostel as yet. It isn't bad but it's noisy at night. Anyway Dad, God bless and take care of yourself. Your loving daughter Jennifer.' And there's a P.S.

KEVIN *enters jangling keys.*

KEVIN: Don't mind me. Oh 'ello, still here Wandsworth? You *are* havin' a long chat about your friend ain't you?

GEORGE: My name's George.

KEVIN (*to* THELMA): Christ gel. You'd never get on the list of the world's best dressed women.

THELMA: You can talk, I've seen

scarecrows better dressed than you.

JOYCE: What are you doing in here? We're in the middle of something important. We've been allocated this highly unsuitable room, now the least you can do is to leave us in peace in it.

KEVIN: I've got to come in here. It's where I keep the harmful chemicals.

He unlocks the store cupboard.

JOYCE: In the crèche?

KEVIN: Don't blame me! It's Horace's doing. I've inherited his system.

He takes a bottle of Harpic powder and a gallon container of bleach out of the cupboard.

JOYCE: Do you realise how dangerous that stuff is? If any child got hold of these containers . . .

KEVIN: I keep it locked don't I? I ain't a fool. Just 'cos I'm doing a menial job it don't mean I ain't got it up here. You shouldn't underestimate the workers Mrs Chalmers. It could land you and your sort in a lot of bother.

JOYCE: What do you mean by 'my sort'?

KEVIN: Well it's the opposite of my sort ain't it?

JOYCE: You're talking about the great class divide are you?

KEVIN: Yeah, that and other things.

THELMA: My mum says that we're all working class now, even the Queen has to work, opening power stations and things.

KEVIN (*mock forgetfulness, hand to forehead*): Course, I keep forgettin', the old working class ain't workin' anymore is it? All you educated people have got the jobs. Course, there's a few of us left to mess around with ballcocks.

THELMA: Do you have to swear? It's not nice is it Mrs Chalmers?

JOYCE: He wasn't swearing Thelma. A ballcock is a technical term, it's part of a cistern.

THELMA: I don't care what system it's part of. I don't like language.

KEVIN: That's 'cos' you're bleedin' ignorant of what language is!

GEORGE: Well we're all here for that reason aren't we? Can we get on?

KEVIN: You ain't got long, I'm locking up in twenty minutes!

He goes to exit.

JOYCE: That's a lethal mixture of chemicals. I hope you've read the instructions on those containers.

KEVIN (*scornful laugh*): It ain't exactly bedside reading is it? (*Mocks.*) Oh what shall I read tonight? Yes, I'll take a bottle of Harpic up with me and snuggle down for a good read. (*Contemptuous laugh.*) Can't stand here chatting, I've got a filthy bog to clean out. One of your posh creative wine tasters has just spewed his guts up. Rather an 'amusing' little vintage. Goodnight, dumbos!

He slams the door and exits. JOYCE *is furious, trembling.*

JOYCE: Try not to let him bother you.

There is lots of displacement activity.

JOYCE: My God! It's no wonder the country's on it's knees! I've always thought of myself as a humanitarian but just lately compulsory euthanasia for teenagers looks an attractive proposition. Don't you agree?

GEORGE (*baffled*): Yes.

THELMA: I didn't understand anything you said.

GEORGE: I got the drift, so to speak. Can we carry on with the letter?

JOYCE: Yes. As I was saying (*she is trying to calm down,*) there's a P.S. (*Reading:*) 'I know you hate writing Dad, but please let me know how you're getting on in London. By the way, Mum doesn't know I am writing to you. It's easier that way.'

JOYCE *folds up the letter.*

GEORGE: So she's all right. (*Pause.*) Thank you. Very nicely read.

JOYCE: So your daughter doesn't know about your difficulties?

GEORGE: No, her mother did all the writing that there was to be done. It made things very awkward for me when my wife remarried . . . Awkward in every which way.

JOYCE: How long have you had the letter?

GEORGE: It's coming up for eight weeks. She'll be getting worried. I haven't been able to reply.

THELMA (*to* JOYCE): He could have sent a telegram. Dictated it. That would have been the sensible thing to do.

GEORGE: Not a telegram! She'd think I'd passed on!

THELMA: She'd know that you hadn't when she opened it!

GEORGE: But it's the first shock. No, not a telegram.

JOYCE: A postcard wouldn't overtax her would it? You could write something like, Everything O.K. Love Dad.

THELMA (*scornfully*): Everything O.K. Love Dad! It's not much of a message to send thousands of miles.

JOYCE: It's better than nothing!

GEORGE: Yes, it says everything I want to say.

THELMA: But he can't write can he?

GEORGE: That's the stumbling block.

JOYCE: I can. I could write it for you.

THELMA: But she'll know it's not his handwriting.

GEORGE: I haven't got any handwriting! (*Pause.*) But it's deceitful isn't it?

JOYCE: It'll stop her worrying.

THELMA: And they do say . . . (*Small pause.*) What the something doesn't know, the something doesn't grieve over.

GEORGE (*not convinced*): Yes.

JOYCE: I've got a postcard somewhere, (*she hunts in her bag*) and a stamp.

THELMA: That's an organiser bag isn't it?

JOYCE: Yes, and I can never find a thing in it.

She finds the postcard and produces it.

GEORGE: It's very colourful. Go on then, yes she'd like that.

THELMA: Ugh, it's modern art. My mother says that chimpanzees could do better.

JOYCE: Your mother knows what she likes, does she Thelma?

Pause.

The address Mr Bishop.

She copies the address from the letter.

THELMA: Yes, she's got firm opinions on most things, she's a bit set in her ways. It's because she's old. She had me late, I was an afterbirth (*Pause.*) She's one of the oldest women in Britain to give birth, she's famous for it in Northampton. I used to fetch her pension on my way home from school. Her home help gets it now.

JOYCE: There you are, Mr Bishop.

GEORGE: Well, that's most kind, and very neat. If I had a copy of *Uncle Tom's Cabin* I'd present you with it. (*Admiring the postcard:*) The bloke who painted this knew his stuff.

JOYCE: Picasso.

GEORGE: Yes. I've heard of him. (*He puts the card away.*)

JOYCE *gets up and walks about the room.*

JOYCE: I want to talk to you for a moment about the learning process. You see, although you both *think* you're illiterate — (*Speaks quickly*:) Ugly word, like illigitimate. You can probably read a lot more than you think. Street names, shop names, brand names like Kelloggs, Persil, Bistow and so on. So we'll start with these very familiar words and then progress to more formal exercises. I want to get away from the formality of the classroom, after all, the classroom failed you once so . . .

GEORGE's *hand is in the air.*

What is it Mr Bishop?

GEORGE: Could I be excused, please Miss?

JOYCE: Mr Bishop, there's no need to . . . Yes of course.

GEORGE *gets up and exits.*

JOYCE: How are you doing? (*She looks.*) Very good! Well done!

THELMA: Can you read the first page of this for me now? (*She picks up the* Janet and John Work Book.) Just teach me the first word.

JOYCE: But what use is a word like Janet going to be to you? You need to know useful words like 'Stop', 'On', 'Off', Etcetera!

THELMA: Etcetera! That's a word I'd never use.

JOYCE: We'll do a deal. You do half a lesson for Davina. All right?

THELMA: All right.

JOYCE (*with book*): This word says Janet. What does it say?

THELMA: Janet! You've just told me!

JOYCE: Now do the same as you did when you traced your surname. This letter says 'J' pronounced 'Juh'. Do you know the alphabet?

THELMA: Of course I do!

JOYCE: Say it for me would you?

THELMA *sings the alphabet song. She gets as far as 'N', when she is interrupted by a loud battering on the door.*

THELMA: It's Mrs Eirenstone. She's found me! She thinks I'm here to do Robotics! Quick, teach me a few steps. Pretend to be my Robotics teacher, please! Please!

She's in complete panic.

JOYCE: All right! Calm down!

JOYCE *opens the door,* GEORGE *falls in with a semi-conscious* KEVIN.

THELMA: Oh that's a relief!

GEORGE: Help me to get him to the table!

JOYCE *and* GEORGE *support* KEVIN.

JOYCE: What have you done to him Mr Bishop?

GEORGE: I've done nought to him. I found him with his head down the lavvy!

They lay KEVIN *on his back on the table, his head overlapping the table facing the audience.*

THELMA: Ugh!

GEORGE: He's had a go at doing himself in!

KEVIN: I ain't!

GEORGE: There's a horrible smell in there, like gas it is. It fair knocked me back.

JOYCE: Kevin, Kevin! Did you use Harpic and bleach in the same lavatory bowl?

KEVIN: I always do. Normally I chuck it in and run back out quick, but the bleedin' door jammed. Next thing I know is old Wandsworth here is leaning over me telling me I've got everything to live for.

JOYCE: You didn't read the instructions did you?

KEVIN: No.

JOYCE: You can't read can you?

KEVIN: No. Not a fucking word.

After a long pause.

KEVIN: 'As anybody got a fag?

THELMA: You mustn't smoke! Your lungs will explode!

JOYCE: You need some fresh air and then you must go home and rest.

KEVIN: No, I've gotta ring the bell for home time.

GEORGE: I can do that, I'm a dab hand at bells.

KEVIN: No, I've gotta lock up.

GEORGE: I can do that an' all! There's nought I like better than having a bunch of keys in my hand.

JOYCE: Let Mr Bishop help Kevin, you ought to rest.

KEVIN *sits slumped on the table, he unclips the keys from his waist.*

KEVIN: Look if the Education find out that I'm . . . that . . .

THELMA: You're illiterate.

KEVIN (*shouting*): All right! That I'm illiterate, I'll lose my job.

JOYCE: None of us will say anything will we?

She turns to GEORGE *and* THELMA.

GEORGE: I won't.

GEORGE *exits and rings the bell.*

JOYCE: Thelma?

THELMA: But he's dangerous isn't he? Who knows what could happen next? He's in charge of the gas and electricity and everything.

Long pause.

JOYCE: Thelma! You wouldn't tell anybody?

The bell rings.

THELMA: I'm going home, I've got to give Rory his ten o'clock feed.

THELMA *puts her coat and hat on.*

JOYCE: Will you be coming next week?

THELMA: I don't know, people like him shouldn't be in charge of things. It's not safe.

She exits.

JOYCE (*comfortingly*): She won't say anything.

KEVIN: An' she ain't gonna write an anonymous letter is she?

JOYCE: No, but give me time. (*Pause.*) How have you been coping with the paperwork?

KEVIN: I ain't been coping. Since Horace went, I've been bunging it in a box.

JOYCE: And trying to forget about it?

KEVIN: Yeah, but it's the first thing I think about when I wake up in the morning. Well the second thing. (*He grins.*)

JOYCE: What sort of paperwork is it?

KEVIN (*irritably*): I dunno, it's all black squiggles to me. (*Small pause.*) It's letters and forms and things. (*Pause.*) I ain't thick! I ain't a genius either, but I ain't thick!

JOYCE (*resignedly*): I know that, go and fetch the papers.

KEVIN: What you gonna do with 'em?

JOYCE: Take them home and read them.

KEVIN *exits.* JOYCE *puts her coat on, packs her books, pencils and flashcards away in her bag. She picks a doll from the shelf, cuddles it for a moment, then tenderly lays it into a doll's cot and covers it over with a blanket. She switches the light off and exits.*

Scene Ten

The cubicle. KEVIN *is wearing an old tweed coat. He stands at the cubicle door holding the box of papers.* JOYCE *enters, he hands the box to* JOYCE.

JOYCE: I'll ring you in the morning. You'll be here?

KEVIN: I'm always 'ere.

JOYCE *starts to leave, she turns back.*

JOYCE: How old are you?

KEVIN: Nineteen.

JOYCE *nods.*

JOYCE: Goodnight.

KEVIN: Night.

JOYCE *exits.* KEVIN *throws darts violently into the notice board.*

KEVIN (*as first dart is thrown*): Interfering! (*as second dart is thrown:*) Stuck up! (*as third dart is thrown, shouts:*) Bitch!

GEORGE *enters hesitantly.*

GEORGE: I've done upstairs.

KEVIN: Thanks. (*He holds his hands out for the keys.*) I'll do the rest. I've got me breath back now.

GEORGE: I thought I'd retain possession of 'em for a bit just while I ask you something.

KEVIN: What?

GEORGE: I've got nowhere to sleep tonight.

KEVIN: So?

GEORGE: I wondered if you knew anywhere, so to speak.

KEVIN: Cheap?

GEORGE: Not so expensive as cheap . . . Free.

KEVIN: No.

GEORGE: *This* is a big place.

KEVIN: But it ain't a doss house.

Small pause.

Give me the keys.

GEORGE: I'd be out early in the morning.

KEVIN: No! I'm in enough bleedin' trouble already, give me the keys, an' then piss off out.

GEORGE: I could assist you in the morning . . . I'm a good worker, there's nothing I like better than good hard work. Me hands have gone soft now, but they'd soon harden up.

KEVIN: It ain't allowed. Go on, get out!

GEORGE (*desperate*): Don't make me threaten you Kevin. I want you to *ask* me to stay.

KEVIN: *You threaten me!* You daft old bugger! I could put you in Stoke Mandeville!

GEORGE: I *don't* want to tell anybody.

Long pause.

KEVIN: Oh *that* kind of threat.

They stare at each other. GEORGE *breaks eye contact.*

GEORGE: I'm sorry. I don't know what came over me. They'd have to tear me tongue out before I'd say ought.

He gives KEVIN *the keys.*

KEVIN: Look, I've gotta be somewhere soon. So find yourself a room right?

GEORGE: Right, thank you. It's very accommodating of you. Why don't *you* learn? Then you could dispense with your bandage.

KEVIN: Yeah, it makes liars of us all don't it?

KEVIN (*starts to exit*): Don't forget the lights!

The main door slams.

Scene Eleven

GEORGE *enters the crèche, he puts the little chairs onto the tables. He opens the sides of the wendy house so that the interior is fully revealed. He gazes in, enraptured, then he crosses the room and switches the lights off.*

ACT TWO

Scene One

Three months later, early morning in the crèche, the wendy house is wide open displaying signs of GEORGE's *occupation, filthy shirts are hanging on a wire coathanger. His alarm clock is on a small table next to a camp bed. His radio is on a little bookshelf, the 'Today' programme is on.* GEORGE *is painting at an easel. The painting depicts the exterior of an ironmonger's shop,* GEORGE *is concentrating hard, the sound of a key in the lock is heard.*
    KEVIN *enters carrying a video recorder box.*

KEVIN: Mornin' Wandsworth!

GEORGE (*turning his head*): Morning Kevin. You're an early worm.

KEVIN (*as he unlocks the store cupboard and puts the video on a shelf*): Yeah, couldn't sleep. I bin up all night.

GEORGE: That's called something. Amnesia! No, I can't remember. Insomnia! That's it! Your an insoniac!

KEVIN: Yeah, some sort of maniac. Klepto probably.

GEORGE: What's in the box?

KEVIN: A video recorder. I'm selling it for a friend.

GEORGE: That's nice of you.

KEVIN: It ain't really. Between you and me I'm a bit of a bastard.

He crosses to look over GEORGE's *shoulder at the painting.*

KEVIN: That's nice.

GEORGE: It's where I used to work. Hetheringtons the ironmongers. You don't know of any jobs going in ironmongery round here do you?

KEVIN: To tell you the truth, I ain't sure what ironmongery is.

GEORGE: It's hardware. Nails, buckets, rawlplugs; you know.

KEVIN: Oh, like a D.I.Y. centre?

GEORGE: Yes, but I want a job in a proper shop where you have a counter and somebody behind it. I used to be a somebody when I was behind that counter. Lovely bit of mahogany it was.

KEVIN: You should've stayed there.

GEORGE: I would have done if Mr Hetherington hadn't died. He understood my difficulties with reading and writing. He used to say, 'George so long as you can put your finger on the stock and manage the money I don't mind'.
But his son! All systems and stock control and serve yourself. It were no good me staying on. I couldn't cope with it. It were humiliating, one day he said to me, 'What's up with you man, can't you read?' I said quietly like, 'No, I can't'. And I put me cap on and went home.

KEVIN: Still you're learnin' now, ain't you?

GEORGE: Ay, forty years too late. But I can write me name and address now.

GEORGE *takes a piece of paper out of his pocket and gives it to* KEVIN.

KEVIN: What's it say?

GEORGE: Mister George Arthur Bishop. The Wendy House.

They laugh.

KEVIN: You'll have to be out soon, the kids'll be here at half eight.

GEORGE: Yes I know, I'll clear up, then I'll be off.

KEVIN: Where you going?

GEORGE: To the Barbican.

KEVIN: What's on?

GEORGE: The central heating, I just go to keep warm. You don't get moved on there you see. It's a big place so you can get lost in it.

Pause.

KEVIN: You got your lesson tonight ain't you?

GEORGE: Yes, so I've got something to look forward to. Right I'd better move. (*He stands.*) Oh me legs are stiff.

KEVIN: Here. (*He feels in his pocket for a coin.*) Go on the bus George, you look knackered.

GEORGE *looks at the fifty pence coin.*

GEORGE: No, the walk'll do me good.

KEVIN: It's pissing down out there and you ain't got a coat. Go on, take it.

GEORGE: No, I've always paid me own way.

KEVIN: You can't pay your own way if you ain't got the money can you?

GEORGE *packs his stuff away.* KEVIN *places the coin on the table in front of him.*

KEVIN: You'll have to start claiming the Social, Wandsworth. You can't live on nothin'. Even the invisible man had his bandages to support him.

GEORGE: No. I'll find some employment soon. And I've still got a few things I can sell.

KEVIN: Like what?

GEORGE: Me clock, and that's a good radio that is. I've had it for years.

KEVIN: You'd be lucky to get a quid for the two, an' how long's that gonna keep you goin'?

GEORGE *pins his picture on the wall.*

GEORGE: Will I be able to impose on you again tonight?

KEVIN: Yeah, why not? Shall you be requiring the Wendy House Suite again Sir, or do you fancy a change? The boiler house is free since Mrs Onassis checked out last night.

GEORGE (*smiling*): No the Wendy House is all right. It's compact.

KEVIN: That's a nice one, 'compact'.

GEORGE: Yes, I heard it on 'Talking About Antiques'. Arther Negus used it in relation to an old tea caddy.

They exit. Blackout.

Scene Two

Later on the same night. The cubicle, KEVIN inside 'reading' the Sun. *JOYCE enters, she has a more dressy image.*

JOYCE: Evening Kevin. (*She lowers her voice.*) Anything for me to do?

KEVIN (*loud voice looking around*): Evenin' Mrs Chalmers. (*He lowers his voice:*) Yeah.

He hands a stack of letters to JOYCE. *JOYCE passes envelopes to* KEVIN.

JOYCE (*shuffling through them*): They're mostly bookings, nothing urgent. Any problem with the replies?

KEVIN: No, but I've 'ad a few compliments on my written English. If I ain't careful, I'm gonna end up bein' promoted to Clerical Officer. You'll have to put a few spelling mistakes in or something.

JOYCE: Kevin, I can't do your paperwork for ever you know.

KEVIN: I know that.

JOYCE: Well, when are you going to think about doing it yourself? It would solve so many of your problems if only you'd learn to read.

KEVIN: No thanks. I'd have to read about every other bleeder's problems then wouldn't I?

JOYCE: Then you'll have to look around for somebody else I'm afraid.

KEVIN: You ain't ditching me are you?

JOYCE: I'm not prepared to help somebody who won't help himself.

So you'd better think about it. (*Pause.*) What are you doing with this?

She picks up the Sun.

KEVIN: I'm looking at the pictures.

JOYCE: Despicable Tory rag!

KEVIN: No it ain't! It's a Socialist paper. It's the paper for the workers. Everybody round our way reads it.

JOYCE (*tersely*): Kevin, this newspaper supports the Conservative Party. It also supports hanging, flogging, fox-hunting, private medicine, cruise missiles, capitalism and Margaret Thatcher. If it dared it would advocate the abolition of the trade unions, the amputation of shoplifters' hands, the castration of homosexuals and the canonisation of Princess Diana. But you wouldn't know that would you? Because you only look at the bloody pictures, because *you can't read!*

KEVIN (*shouting*): I don't wanna read about life. I wanna live it!

JOYCE: All right live it! But from now on you'll live it without my help.

JOYCE exits angrily towards the crèche.
KEVIN tears the Sun *to pieces. He throws it all over the floor, then lights a fag and leans against the wall.*

Scene Three

The crèche. JOYCE *is taking off her coat,* THELMA *is wearing her dance gear.*

JOYCE: Thelma I can't waste valuable time on it! We only have two hours a week.

THELMA: Just five minutes. Oh, go on! (*She sulks.*) I only want you to stand there and tell me if I'm going wrong.

JOYCE: Why don't you tell Mrs Eirenstone the truth, instead of all these lies?

THELMA: I can't suddenly start telling the truth to people can I? Where would it all end? Please! I have to show her my dance steps when I get back. She says I've got a terrible technique, and she knows what she's talking about, she's started going to Covent Garden, she's talking of complaining to my Robotics teacher, and if she comes here and goes upstairs, I'll be found to be an illiterate liar.

JOYCE: Aerobics! How many more times? And you're not illiterate, you can read and write your own name now, you did last week.

THELMA: Go on! *He's* not here yet. He's probably rooting around in litter bins.

JOYCE: That's cruel. The poor man's just down on his luck. All right, just until he comes.

THELMA *takes a tape cassette out of her bag and switches it on to play loud fast dance exercise music. She hands* JOYCE *an exercise manual.*

THELMA (*shouting over row*): Look in the book and tell me if I'm doing it right.

THELMA *goes into clumsy unco-ordinated dance exercise routine.* GEORGE *enters unnoticed, he has walked a long way and is tired and hungry. Nobody sees* GEORGE, *he sits down on a floor cushion.*

JOYCE (*shouts*): Try to keep to the rhythm Thelma. (*She claps her hands to the beat.*) Like this.

JOYCE *joins in the routine. She does quite well, and enjoys it.* GEORGE *taps his hand and foot to the beat.* KEVIN *opens the door.*

KEVIN (*shouting*): Turn it down!

They all turn to look at KEVIN, JOYCE *hurries to turn the volume down.*

KEVIN: I've had a complaint from 'Positive Thinking'. They reckon they can't concentrate wiv that row goin' on.

JOYCE: Well kindly tell them that their constant chanting of 'I can' and 'I will' has filtered into our room more than once.

KEVIN: Oh I ain't getting involved, do what you like.

KEVIN *exits and slams door.*

GEORGE: Sorry I'm late, I got held up.

THELMA: What, mugged, held up?

GEORGE: No, detained, held up.

JOYCE: Did you manage to do your homework Mr Bishop?

GEORGE: Yes.

He brings a sheath of papers out of a plastic carrier and hands them to JOYCE.

JOYCE: These are beautifully neat George, well done!

GEORGE: I enjoyed it. It passed the time very constructively.

GEORGE *smiles.*

JOYCE: Did you manage to do yours Thelma?

THELMA: Yes, but I couldn't bring it with me. Mrs Eirenstone pinned it up on the cork tiles in the nursery. She thinks Davina's done it. I could hardly tell her it was mine could I? (*Bitterly:*) So Davina's getting all *my* credit. Mr Eirenstone took her to see *Peter Pan* on account of it. But it was me who was up all night with her. If she wasn't screaming about the crocodile, she was in hysterics over Captain Luck.

JOYCE: Hook! 'aitch', huh!

She writes it on a piece of card.

GEORGE (*to* THELMA): It looks like a ladder wi' one rung.

THELMA: Mrs Chalmers is the teacher, not you.

THELMA *looks at* GEORGE's *homework.*

THELMA: He's doing much better than me. He's making rapid progress.

GEORGE: Well you've got those kiddies to look after. They can be very consuming of time.

THELMA: Davina's had a smack from me, she's getting out of hand. Mrs Eirenstone blames me for it, but how can it be my fault? She's not my flesh and blood is she? She won't sit down and do her letters practice. I say to her 'Davina you won't go to that nice school that your Mummy's found if you don't learn your letters'. She says some horrible things back to me. Swear words you know. She hears it from Mr Eirenstone.

JOYCE (*trying to interrupt the flow*): You mustn't pressure Davina! Thelma, she's only a little child.

THELMA: It's me that's under pressure! It's me that does all the housework and looks after Davina, and the baby, and now Mr and Mrs Eirenstone are both on at me to write down telephone messages. (*Tearful:*) I can't remember who's who. They should answer their own phone instead of lying in bed all day!

GEORGE: So you're not happy in your work?

THELMA: I was employed to look after the children, but I've ended up washing Mr Eirenstone's silk underpants by hand! In fact I have to do all the washing by hand.

JOYCE: Surely they've got a washing machine?

THELMA: Yes, but I can't work it. Mrs Eirenstone gave me the instruction book and left me to get on with it. It's the same with the freezer, I don't know what the labels say. I have to defrost everything to see what it is then freeze it up again. Oh I wish I lived a hundred years ago, you didn't need to read then. You could just live your life in peace.

JOYCE: In ignorance.

THELMA: It's the same thing.

GEORGE: Oh no it isn't. When you're ignorant the clever people take advantage of you. They tell you what to do, and you have to do it. You don't know how to refuse, because you don't know the words.

KEVIN *enters.*

KEVIN: Don't mind if I come in do you?

JOYCE: Kevin, these constant interruptions are very unsettling. What is it this time?

KEVIN: I just wanted somewhere to get out of the way. 'Paper Sculpture' are after me for chuckin' their poxy models in the bin.

He sits crossed-legged on the floor.

JOYCE: You didn't! Oh dear, there'll be a few tears shed under the duvet tonight!

KEVIN: How was I to know they wanted 'em saving? The hairy ponce of a tutor said he put a notice against 'em. 'Do not throw away'. He went bleedin' berserk when he found that in the bin.

JOYCE: But why come in here? Why don't you barge into someone else's class?

KEVIN *starts to roll a fag.*

KEVIN: Nobody else would have me. Carry on, pretend I'm not here.

THELMA *looks resentfully at* KEVIN, GEORGE *smiles at him.*

JOYCE (*sighs*): We're going on with the game we played last week. I'm going to hold up a letter and you have to try and find a word that begins with it.

She sorts out 'D' and holds it up.

This is 'D' what sound does it make?

KEVIN: Duh! (*He laughs and holds his fingers to his head and adopts an idiot expression.*

JOYCE: Good, so I want a word beginning with Duh.

GEORGE: Daughter.

JOYCE: Yes.

THELMA (*shouts*): Dog!

JOYCE: Good.

THELMA *is pleased and claps her hands together.*

GEORGE: Down and out.

JOYCE: Yes, but that's three words. But 'Down' is good. Thelma?

THELMA (*triumphantly*): Davina!

GEORGE: Well done!

JOYCE: George another one?

GEORGE: Er . . . Dirt!

JOYCE: Yes.

KEVIN: Drip, drop, doom, day, damned.

THELMA: You're not supposed to be playing.

GEORGE (*admiringly*): But he's got the hang of it.

JOYCE: Any more Kevin?

KEVIN *stands and wanders around.*

KEVIN: Doughnut, drawers, doors, detention.

GEORGE: Disgrace.

THELMA: Dot.

JOYCE: Go on. Whenever you think of one.

GEORGE: Dosser, dirty . . .

THELMA: You said dirty before!

GEORGE: I said dirt before. Dirty is different . . .

THELMA (*triumphantly*): Different!

JOYCE: Very good! Now another letter.

She sorts out 'F' *looks at* KEVIN, *puts it away and takes out* 'B'.

GEORGE: 'B' pronounced Buh!

JOYCE: Yes, go on, a word.

GEORGE: Busby, Barclay.

THELMA: Ball!

GEORGE: Barbican!

KEVIN: Bugger, bollocks, bleedin' bastard.

THELMA *covers her ears.*

JOYCE (*shouting angrily*): Stop it!

THELMA: You shouldn't let him play!

KEVIN: I got it right didn't I?

GEORGE: You mustn't swear in front of the ladies.

THELMA: Tell him to get out.

JOYCE: He *did* get them right, they weren't words that I would have chosen, but . . .

KEVIN: Barrel, barometer, butter, bacon, beans, bread.

GEORGE: Better!

KEVIN: Beano.

JOYCE: We'll have another letter now.

She sorts another letter out.

KEVIN: Bottle, beer, brewery.

JOYCE: Thank you, we'll have another letter now.

KEVIN *walks around the room.*

KEVIN: Beautiful, barmy, barnacle, barn, bastard.

THELMA: You've had that one!

KEVIN: Which one?

THELMA: The last one you said.

KEVIN: Book, bag, bouncer, bounce.

JOYCE: Thank you Kevin.

KEVIN: Banana, bullet (*Proudly:*) *Barrage Balloon.*

GEORGE *and* JOYCE *applaud,* THELMA *is jealous.*

JOYCE: Excellent.

KEVIN: Do I get a gold star?

JOYCE (*pleased*): Yes, why not? There are bound to be some around here somewhere.

JOYCE *searches.*

GEORGE: You're a clever lad. How come you've heard of barrage balloons? I'd have thought the generation gap would have intervened so to speak.

KEVIN: Me Grandma used to talk for hours about the war. How happy they were queuing for their bits of bacon.

THELMA: You mean unhappy!

KEVIN: No I mean happy. Still what else happened in her life? Her next highlight was havin' her veins done in hospital.

JOYCE *finds a tin of gold stars.*

JOYCE (*taking one out*): Where do you want it?

KEVIN (*mock dramatic*): Stick it here. (*Indicates his forehead.*) That way everybody can see it, and know that Kevin Muldoon is a gold star winner.

JOYCE *sticks it on his forehead.*

THELMA: Don't I get one?

JOYCE: Of course, you've *all* done well.

JOYCE *gives a gold star to* THELMA. THELMA *puts it into her purse.*

JOYCE: And you George.

GEORGE: I'll have it on my homework please.

JOYCE *sticks it on his homework book.*

GEORGE: First time I've had one of these. The highest I got at school was a red. (*Pause.*) I got that for a drawing of a cut up frog.

KEVIN: I've never liked the French either.

GEORGE: I used to draw when the others were writing.

JOYCE: I could never draw a straight line. I envy anyone with that skill.

GEORGE: I wouldn't call it a skill, but I used to enjoy it. I had a very envious collection of coloured pencils. They came in tins with pictures of lakes on them. I used to lay them on my bed and gloat over 'em. I were like a miser with his money.

He gives a small laugh.

KEVIN: I collected foreign fag packets. My big sister knocked about with all sorts.

Pause.

She collected three kids, different colours though, so you couldn't call 'em a set.

JOYCE: What about you Thelma? What did you collect?

THELMA: Pictures of dogs. I love all living things.

KEVIN: What about you Mrs Charmer?

JOYCE: Chalmers.

KEVIN: I know what I said, what filled your empty hours?

JOYCE: Oh, I've always been a great reader.

She realises the gaffe.

KEVIN: Go on, rub it in.

JOYCE: I collected books. (*Pause.*) Now it's time for some practical work.

JOYCE *starts to sort out papers.*

KEVIN: You're a bit cagey ain't you Mrs Chalmers?

JOYCE: What do you mean?

KEVIN: You take it all in, but you don't give nothin' out do you? Where do you live?

JOYCE: In Clapham.

KEVIN: On the common? Big house? Five bedrooms?

JOYCE: Yes.

KEVIN: Servants?

JOYCE: Don't be silly.

KEVIN: Domestic help?

JOYCE: A cleaning lady. And somebody comes in to mow the lawn.

KEVIN: *Somebody!* You're married ain't you?

JOYCE: Yes.

KEVIN: Happy?

JOYCE: That's none of your business.

KEVIN: What's your old man do?

JOYCE: He's a G.P.

KEVIN: A doctor eh? That must come in handy.

GEORGE: He likes opera, we know that much.

THELMA: Have you got any children of your own?

JOYCE: No.

THELMA: Have you been trying for some?

JOYCE: No, not lately.

THELMA: Is it you or him?

JOYCE: Me or him what?

THELMA: That's sterile?

JOYCE: It's neither of us.

THELMA: But if you can't have a baby it must be somebody's fault.

JOYCE: It's not a question of fault.

THELMA: Has your husband done the tests on you?

JOYCE: He certainly has not!

THELMA: Why not? Then you'd know who to blame. What about adoption? With your husband being a doctor you could have your pick of the orphanages. Why don't you put your name down? You wouldn't have to wait long.

GEORGE: That's enough Thelma!

JOYCE: Yes, we're losing valuable time!

KEVIN: What are you doing this for?

JOYCE: I'm not doing it am I? You're preventing me from doing it.

KEVIN: All right I'll go.

JOYCE: You don't have to go! You know we'd like you to join the class.

KEVIN: No, this room gives me the creeps. I shit myself first day at school. I spent the whole of the morning stuck to one of them little chairs.

THELMA (*gets up quickly from her chair*): Ugh!

KEVIN *exits.*

JOYCE: I'm sorry about that.

GEORGE: It's just a phrase he's going through.

He takes an air-mail letter out.

GEORGE: I've had another letter, would you mind?

THELMA: I'm sure you won't mind if *I* go out will you?

JOYCE *takes the letter with an air of resignation, sits down and reads it.*

JOYCE: Dear Dad . . .

Blackout.

Scene Four

At the cubby hole. KEVIN *is sweeping the torn papers up.* THELMA *enters.*

KEVIN: What you doing out of class?

THELMA: She's reading one of his daughter's boring letters. She ignores me when he's around.

KEVIN: She's in love with him ain't she?

THELMA: Of course not. She's married to a doctor.

KEVIN: Don't mean she can't have a bit on the side.

THELMA: With that dirty old man!

KEVIN: Some women like dirty old men. It turns 'em on.

THELMA: You're the most horrible person I've ever met.

KEVIN: You've had a sheltered life though, ain't you?

THELMA: I was brought up properly,

if that's what you mean. There was no dirty talk in our family.

KEVIN: What did you talk about apart from lovin' all livin' things?

THELMA: The usual things that families talk about: television, illness, what to have for dinner.

KEVIN: You didn't discuss philosophy then?

THELMA: I don't know what philosophy is and neither do you. You're like George Bishop, you are. You use these words that you can't read and you can't write and try to make people think you're clever. Well it doesn't work with me.

KEVIN: What you goin' to do when you can read then?

THELMA: Mrs Chalmers says my whole life will change.

KEVIN: You gonna carry on being a nanny?

THELMA: Yes, for a few years until I've had my fling.

KEVIN: When you havin' that then?

THELMA: I'm having it now. What do you think I'm in London for?

KEVIN: Then what?

THELMA: Get married of course.

KEVIN: Who to?

THELMA: *I* don't know. I'm not a fortune teller am I? But there's bound to be somebody out there waiting for me isn't there?

KEVIN: Yeah, the Wandsworth Wanker.

He laughs. THELMA *goes to rush off.*

KEVIN: Oi Thelma!

THELMA: What?

KEVIN: You ever had a bloke?

THELMA: What do you mean?

KEVIN: Ever had a boyfriend?

THELMA: No, I'm saving myself.

KEVIN: What for?

THELMA: The right man.

KEVIN: How will you know when you've found him?

THELMA: Because I'll fall in love with him stupid! And he'll fall in love with me.

KEVIN (*acting*): Thelma do you think you could love me?

THELMA: No!

KEVIN: Thelma.

THELMA: What?

KEVIN: I love you gel.

THELMA: No you don't, you're a liar. A born liar.

KEVIN: No straight up. I've been trying to keep it to myself but I gotta tell you. Thelma. Come to Kevin. Come on.

THELMA comes closer.

THELMA: What for?

KEVIN: Thelma. Luh is for love. Luh. Love.

He puts his arms around her, he pulls her towards him.

KEVIN: Kuh is for kiss. Kuh. Kiss.

He kisses her on the cheek.

KEVIN: Duh is for Darlin'. Duh. Darlin'. Buh is for Bosom.

THELMA: What's that?

KEVIN: It's a fancy word for tits.

He grasps her breasts, THELMA *screams and pushes him off.*

THELMA: To think that Jesus gave his life to save the likes of you!

THELMA *runs off towards the lavatory.*

Scene Five

In the crèche. JOYCE *is rocking*
GEORGE *to and fro.* GEORGE *is holding
the letter, he is upset.*

JOYCE: Children are always a worry
aren't they?

GEORGE: I can't bear to think of her so
unhappy and so far away. It's not as if
I can get on a bus is it? You can't,
not to Australia. I'd kill that Malcolm
if I got my hands on him.

JOYCE: There, there. If she's so unhappy
with him, she may decide to come
back.

GEORGE: I wish she would. You've no
idea how much I miss her, she's such
a lovely girl. She'd do anything for
anybody. You could warm your hands
on her heart.

A long pause.

JOYCE: I had a son. He'll be nineteen on
the fourteenth of December. His name
was Robert.

GEORGE: Nice.

JOYCE: A gentle name.

GEORGE: It would have been shortened.

JOYCE: Yes.

GEORGE: He went ahead and died did
he?

JOYCE: He was a very singular baby. The
nurses said that they had never quite
seen anything like him before. I wasn't
allowed to see him, but by all accounts
he had arms and legs all over the place.
(*Pause.*) My husband won't have his
name mentioned. He'd be at
university by now. (*Pause.*) I look
at them in the streets.

GEORGE *cuddles* JOYCE *and strokes
her hair.*

GEORGE: I wish we could be friends
Mrs Chalmers.

JOYCE: We are friends Mr Bishop.

GEORGE: No, we're friendly, but we're
not friends.

THELMA *enters. She sees* GEORGE
and JOYCE *with their arms around
each other.* GEORGE *and* JOYCE
get to their feet.

THELMA: It's too late, I saw you!

JOYCE: Mr Bishop has had some
upsetting news.

THELMA: Well I'm upset. I've just
been indecently assaulted, but
nobody puts their arms around me
do they?

GEORGE: Who assaulted you? Not the
Wandsworth . . .

THELMA: No! That caretaker!

She cries. JOYCE *puts her arms
around her.*

JOYCE: He's gone too far this time.
What did he do to you?

THELMA *looks at* GEORGE.

THELMA: He touched me here. (*She
indicates her breasts.*) He said he
loved me, then he did it.

JOYCE: They always say they love you.
It's their way.

THELMA: But I don't want anybody
to touch me there. Not until I'm
married. He said you're in love with
him. (*She looks at* GEORGE.) It's
not true is it?

JOYCE: No, of course it's not true!
He's a nasty malicious boy to say that.

THELMA: You *looked* as if you were
in love with him when I came in.

GEORGE *looks at* JOYCE, *she
looks at him.*

JOYCE: Mr Bishop and I are friends.

GEORGE: Yes, we're friends. (*He looks
pleased.*)

THELMA: But you do a lot for him
don't you?

JOYCE: I hope I give you both the
same amount of time.

THELMA: You do more for him.

JOYCE: That's not true.

THELMA: That's why he's learning quicker than me.

JOYCE: He has more time for practice.

GEORGE: I haven't got a job. I'm free in the day.

THELMA: No, you like him better than me.

JOYCE: I like you both equally.

THELMA (*shouting*): Don't tell lies! You've never liked me!

JOYCE: Stop shouting.

THELMA (*louder*): I'll shout as loud as I like! Mrs Eirenstone does, so why shouldn't I? She throws things about. (*She throws flash cards on the floor.*) And nobody tells her to stop. You don't post my letters.

JOYCE: You don't write any.

THELMA: You don't kiss me!

JOYCE (*quietly*): I can do. (*She kisses her.*)

JOYCE: Do you want me to come and see Mrs Eirenstone?

THELMA: What about?

JOYCE: You're not happy there are you? She's not treating you well.

THELMA: I haven't had any wages for two weeks.

JOYCE: How much does she owe you?

THELMA: Forty pounds.

JOYCE: So eighty pounds in all. (*Pause.*) That's not much for two weeks' work!

THELMA: No, she owes me forty pounds for two weeks.

JOYCE: She can't be paying you twenty pounds a week!

THELMA: And my board. Mrs Eirenstone says it's what everyone gets on Youth Opportunities.

GEORGE: Doesn't sound like much of an opportunity to me.

JOYCE: She's lying to you. A trained nanny wouldn't warm a bottle for twenty pounds a week.

THELMA: Well I'm not trained am I? So she can pay me what she likes.

GEORGE: We're not at liberty to pick and choose Mrs Chalmers.

JOYCE: I know that, but you will be, you're learning.

GEORGE: No we've never been able to choose, we've always done as we're told.

THELMA: I could have him up for indecent assault couldn't I? What he's done is against the law. I'm going to report him to the police.

JOYCE: No, don't do anything hasty.

GEORGE: You'd have to go to court.

JOYCE: It'd be in the papers. 'Literacy Student Assaulted by School Caretaker'.

GEORGE: Mrs Eirenstone would find out.

THELMA: He ought to be punished!

She puts her hat and coat on.

JOYCE: Where are you going?

THELMA: Back to Kensington.

JOYCE: You haven't finished your lesson!

THELMA: I don't care! I've had enough for tonight.

JOYCE: Are you coming next week?

THELMA: I don't know. I might. I might not!

GEORGE: Next Wednesday is bonfire night.

JOYCE: Is it? Oh dear, I'm meant to be hostessing at a bonfire party. It's our turn to have the black patch on the lawn.

GEORGE: Does that mean there won't be a lesson next week?

THELMA: She's just said she's going to a party instead of coming here.

JOYCE: My husband arranged it. You see

it's my birthday as well. He'll be awfully cross if . . .

THELMA: Will you be here or won't you?

Pause.

JOYCE: I'll be here.

KEVIN *stands at the open door.*
THELMA *exits, ignoring* KEVIN.

GEORGE: I'll walk her to the bus, she's too upset to be out there on her own.

GEORGE *exits, passing* KEVIN.

GEORGE (*to* KEVIN): You want to learn to keep yourself in check. I know your hormones are churning round, but young Thelma's a decent girl, and now Mrs Chalmers is upset.

JOYCE *is slumped depressed. The door opens quietly and* KEVIN *enters.*

KEVIN: What's up Joyce? George says you're upset. Tell Kevin.

JOYCE: Please call me Mrs Chalmers from now on.

KEVIN: Mrs Charmer, I call you that 'cos your charmin' ain't you?

JOYCE: No!

KEVIN: You are.

JOYCE: Go away Kevin. I'm not in the mood.

KEVIN: I'm always in the mood. I had a thing about Mrs Thatcher last year. I couldn't see a navy blue tailored suit without sitting down and crossing my legs.

JOYCE: Kevin. I won't allow you in here if you carry on talking like that.

KEVIN: I can't help it if I've got a crush on you. Can I?

JOYCE (*drily*): It'll pass.

KEVIN: I know, but how long will it take, that's the 'fing?

JOYCE: So you find me attractive, do you?

KEVIN: Yeah. I go for older women.

They've got better bodies. Softer you know. Younger birds is all knees and elbows.

JOYCE: How many older women have you had?

KEVIN: Well it's hard to say.

JOYCE: Twelve?

KEVIN: No, not twelve.

JOYCE: One?

KEVIN: Something in between.

JOYCE: And how many young girls?

KEVIN: Look I ain't going into detail.

JOYCE: Would you like to come home with me tonight Kevin?

KEVIN: What for?

JOYCE: Well, let's call it . . . coffee, shall we?

KEVIN: Won't your husband mind?

JOYCE: My husband's not there, he's gone to a conference on herpes. We could get to know each other intimately.

KEVIN: You dirty old bag!

JOYCE: You clean young virgin! You touch Thelma again and I'll bloody castrate you!

She holds up a pair of scissors.

Snip! Snip!

KEVIN *runs from the room.* JOYCE *laughs.*

Scene Six

The crèche, the following week. A model of a guy sits slumped over the table. It is a good facsimile of a human being. It is wearing GEORGE's *best clothes.*

After five seconds, the door is unlocked and KEVIN *and* GEORGE *enter.* GEORGE *is wearing his oldest outdoor clothes, and looks like a tramp.*

He is carrying a large thin greetings card box. KEVIN *is carrying a step ladder.*

KEVIN: We'll have to get a move on.

He sees the guy.

Bleedin' 'ell! That it?

GEORGE (*going to guy and picking it up*): I were up all night constructing him. What do you think?

KEVIN: He's better dressed than you are George.

GEORGE: He's got my best clothes on that's why!

KEVIN: Where'd you get the money from for that card?

GEORGE: I sold me wireless. It'll be the first time I've missed *The Archers* for I don't know how long. Now I shall never know how Phil got his muck spreader out of that ditch. (*Pause.*) Still it'll be worth it when she sees it. Big i'nt it?

He opens the box and looks at the card, the card says 'To my sweetheart'.

KEVIN: She's forty-six ain't she?

KEVIN *puts the step ladder in the middle of the room.*

GEORGE: Yes, but they didn't have one with forty-six on. They stop at twenty-one.

KEVIN: I hope she appreciates all this.

GEORGE: Oh she will. She's an appreciative type of woman. In fact she's the nicest woman I've ever met. So to speak.

GEORGE *hands* KEVIN *a hanging structure that is decorated with cut out Halloween shapes.*
As KEVIN *hangs decorations:*

KEVIN: What about your wife?

GEORGE: Oh I liked her but she got fed up with me. I didn't push myself forward enough with her. It's a general fault I've got. She said I was boring.

KEVIN: Never!

GEORGE: Well you see she was always a lively sort of woman. Always laughing.

KEVIN: Bit of a goer eh?

GEORGE: Yes, she was always on the go. She had a thirst for amusement. I thought she might slow down a bit when Jennifer was born, but she was worse than ever. Rumours started circulating, I took no notice. (*Pause.*) You see, looking after the baby wasn't enough for her, didn't satisfy her brain. She wanted to meet people and have them tell her she looked pretty. (*Pause.*) I told her. Twenty or more times a day, but it wasn't enough, so I brought up Jennifer. She was a daddy's girl. I got as much pleasure from seeing her clean after her bath as ever I got from watching Sheffield score at home.

Long pause.

KEVIN: George?

GEORGE: Yes?

KEVIN: You don't half stink, me old flower.

GEORGE (*hanging his head*): I've let myself go a bit lately . . .

KEVIN: No offence.

GEORGE: No, none taken.

Pause as they hang decorations.

GEORGE: I heard a new word today.

KEVIN: Yeah?

GEORGE: Serendipity. Lovely isn't it? (*Slowly:*) Serendipity.

KEVIN: What's it mean?

GEORGE: I don't know. I just came across it.

KEVIN *looks at his watch.*

KEVIN: I gotta unlock the front door for Thelma.

GEORGE: How long will you be?

KEVIN: Five minutes.

He climbs down the stepladder and closes it up.

GEORGE (*anxiously*): You're going to apologise to her aren't you for last week?

KEVIN: Yeah, I'll think of something.

GEORGE: Good.

KEVIN *goes towards door with the stepladder.*

GEORGE: Better lock me in. We don't want Joyce to come in before we're ready.

KEVIN: George.

GEORGE: Yes?

KEVIN: If I were you I wouldn't get too fond of Mrs Charmer.

GEORGE: It's her birthday!

KEVIN: Yeah. And it's bonfire night an'll but you ain't gonna light her fire George.

KEVIN *exits and locks the door.*

GEORGE *takes his clothes off, revealing newspaper padding and tattered underwear. He takes water from the goldfish bowl with a jam jar, then using a corner of his towel he washes under his arms, his face and neck. He hears voices in the corridor outside, he freezes, then panics when he hears the key in the lock. He runs into the wendy house taking his clothes.*

THELMA *and* KEVIN *enter,* KEVIN *looks round for* GEORGE. THELMA *is carrying a cake in a tupperware box.*

THELMA (*looking around*): Ah look what the kiddies have done! What's wrong with *him?*

KEVIN *lights the pumpkin lamps.*

KEVIN: Wandsworth (*indicating guy*) ain't 'at his best tonight. I told him to get his head down for a bit.

THELMA: *Look* at him, he looks like a tramp. In fact he *is* a tramp.

KEVIN: Oh he ain't a bad guy.

He laughs.

THELMA (*suspicious*): What are you laughing for? You're not going to go funny again are you?

KEVIN (*acting*): I explained all that Thelma. I wasn't myself last week.

THELMA: You should have told me about your whole family dying in a plane crash last year. It must have been awful for you remembering. I would have made allowances. Where were they going?

KEVIN: Who?

THELMA: Your family.

KEVIN: Oh er . . . South of France for the sunshine.

THELMA: In November?

KEVIN: Look I can't talk about it no more, sorry.

THELMA (*anxiously*): I wish you'd told me last week. I wouldn't have been so mad.

KEVIN: It doesn't matter.

THELMA: It does!

THELMA *takes the lid off the cake box.* GEORGE *exits from Wendy House, he is wearing a bow tie.* THELMA *sees him and screams.*

GEORGE: Sorry, I couldn't come out before I weren't properly dressed.

KEVIN *laughs.*

THELMA: I don't think it's funny. People have nearly died of shocks like that. I could have ended up in intensive care with a tube up my nose.

KEVIN: Show George the cake you made Thelma. I gotta open up.

THELMA *brings* GEORGE *the cake,* KEVIN *exits.*

GEORGE: Yes, it's very nice but you've spelt happy wrong. Happy's spelt with two 'Ps'.

THELMA: She won't mind.

GEORGE: I think she will.

THELMA: No she won't, she'll be grateful to me for standing in the kitchen all day while Davina's been under my feet having tantrums on the cushion floor.

GEORGE: Put another P on Thelma, you've got enough silver balls.

THELMA: No it'll ruin it and anyway it doesn't matter.

GEORGE: It does matter! That's not how you spell happy. (*He sings*:) I'm H.A.P.P.Y. H.A.P.P.Y. Please Thelma, before she comes. I'll do it if you like.

He tries to hold the cake.

THELMA: No it's my cake. Leave it alone . . . so long as it tastes all right . . .

GEORGE: But she's not a cookery teacher, she teaches the English language. She won't care what it *tastes* like so long as it's spelt right.

Three knocks on the door.

It's Joyce, light the candle!

THELMA *lights the candle*. GEORGE *switches the main light off, the pumpkin glows in the dark, the single candle flame flares.*

Come in.

JOYCE *and* KEVIN *enter*. KEVIN, THELMA *and* GEORGE *sing 'Happy birthday to you'.* JOYCE *stands overwhelmed. She is wearing an elegant dress, high heels and fur coat.*

JOYCE: How lovely! Thank you!

THELMA: I made the cake. (*Bossily*:) Blow the candle out then!

JOYCE *blows, they applaud,* KEVIN *whistles.*

GEORGE: And I made the guy.

GEORGE *picks it up and holds it.*

KEVIN: An' I got the decorations back from out the bin.

JOYCE: How kind of you all to remember.

KEVIN: George set it up. That's George on the right.

JOYCE: It's a splendid guy.

THELMA: It should have a cloak and a pointed hat by rights.

THELMA *unpacks her handbag and takes out her 'Janet and John' exercise book.*

GEORGE: We thought we'd have our lesson and then have a party. Only a bit of one. A piece of cake and then burn the guy. Kevin's got a sort of bonfire built in the playground.

JOYCE: Well of course that *would* have been lovely. But I have to leave earlier than usual, we've got people coming, I did say last week . . .

GEORGE (*disappointed*): Oh!

KEVIN (*sarcastically*): Oh well, if you've got *people* comin' . . .

JOYCE: Perhaps if we have a *short* lesson . . .

THELMA: But I need a *proper* lesson, I want you to teach me to read this, I've got to read it to Davina tomorrow.

She shows the book to JOYCE.

JOYCE: Would you mind taking a back seat tonight Mr Bishop?

KEVIN: No, he don't mind, do you George. He's used to it ain't you?

GEORGE: Yes, I can get on and do something by myself but I would like a confidential word during the duration.

KEVIN: See you in a bit then?

KEVIN *exits.*

JOYCE, THELMA *and* GEORGE *settle down at the table.* GEORGE *opens an exercise book and reads it to himself moving his lips.*

JOYCE (*reading*): Mother must do this.

THELMA: The washing up.

JOYCE (*reading*): Then she may go out.

(*Pause.*) Good God, that can't be right.

THELMA: Yes it is, look, she's got her coat on.

JOYCE (*reading*): The man must do this.

THELMA: He's sitting at a desk.

JOYCE (*angrily reading*): And then he will do this. It's outrageous!

THELMA: He's sitting in a comfy chair reading the paper, what's wrong with that?

JOYCE: But don't you see Thelma? Mother *must* do this.

GEORGE (*looking at book*): The washing up.

JOYCE: And then, and only then, may she go out!

THELMA: So? My mother always does the washing up before she goes out. And so will I when I get my own kitchen sink.

JOYCE: But *must* Thelma? *Must?*

THELMA: Somebody has to wash up.

JOYCE: But why is it always bloody Mother?

THELMA: Because bloody Daddy's at work! Look!

She jabs her finger on the illustration.

JOYCE: You mustn't let Davina near this, it's years out of date.

THELMA: No it's not! Mrs Eirenstone bought it yesterday, so there!

GEORGE: Daddies do wash up. I used to do all the housework. I got called a big Jessy for doing it an' all.

JOYCE: Who by?

GEORGE: Other men. I got caught ironing once, a rumour went round Huddersfield that I was a poof.

THELMA (*to* JOYCE): I'm in a bad mood now. (*Small pause.*) I don't want to do anymore. (*She pushes the book away.*)

JOYCE: Please yourself. Would you like to see if Kevin's available? We can start the party.

THELMA: You mean get it over with don't you?

THELMA *exits.*

JOYCE: You wanted a word with me George?

GEORGE *gets up, goes into the wendy house and comes out with the card.*

GEORGE: Happy Birthday!

He gives her the box.

JOYCE (*opening it*): Mr Bishop! It's so big! (*Pause.*) Oh!

GEORGE: What's up?

JOYCE (*lying*): Nothing, it's lovely . . . satin . . . hearts and beautifully written. 'All my love from Mr Bishop.' (*Abstracted*:) There's an 'E' on the end of love by the way.

GEORGE: You like it then?

JOYCE (*lying*): Oh yes, it's the biggest and best card I've ever had. (*Reluctantly*:) It's just that, I don't think my husband will be as delighted as I am.

GEORGE: Oh *him.* It's nought to do with him is it?

JOYCE: It says 'Sweetheart', you see 'To my Sweetheart'. (*Indicating*:) He may not understand.

GEORGE: Don't show it to him then. Keep it in a drawer.

JOYCE: It won't fit in a drawer.

There is an awkward pause.

GEORGE: You *are* my sweetheart. (*Small pause.*) So to speak.

JOYCE: But I'm not, I'm your teacher. You must get it straight. I can see it's difficult for you.

Pause.

You've probably never had such a close non-sexual relationship with a woman before have you?

GEORGE: No, all the relationships I've ever had have been with relations.

JOYCE: There you are then, you're transferring all your affection onto me because I'm here every week helping you and interested in you.

GEORGE: So you are *interested* in me?

JOYCE: Of course, in a student-teacher sort of way.

GEORGE: Nothing else?

JOYCE: No, anything else is quite out of the question.

GEORGE: You're not happy with *him* are you?

JOYCE: I don't expect to be *happy* with him. We've been married for twenty-nine years.

GEORGE: You're not seeing me at my best.

JOYCE: It's got nothing to do with how you look or speak.

GEORGE: I said nought about speaking.

JOYCE: No.

GEORGE: What's wrong with how I speak?

JOYCE: Nothing, a northern accent is delightful.

GEORGE: Ar, up North but not down here.

Small pause.

I wish I'd said nought now. I don't know what's up wi' me carrying on, speaking my mind.

JOYCE: You're lonely, you should try to make some friends.

GEORGE: I haven't got the knack.

Pause.

This transferring, does it wear off . . . evaporate?

JOYCE (*eagerly*): Oh yes. It gets transferred to someone else.

KEVIN *and* THELMA *are heard off.*

GEORGE: Right, I'll not speak of it again.

JOYCE: No, best not to, it could make things very difficult.

KEVIN *and* THELMA *enter.*

THELMA: Kevin's been promoted!

KEVIN *is excited. He brings a letter out of his pocket and waves it around.*

KEVIN: I only knew just now. A bloke came round from the Education. He gives me this and says, 'I s'pose you bin expecting this'.

JOYCE: What are you promoted to?

KEVIN: Head caretaker! There ain't nowhere else to go.

GEORGE: Well I think that's grand, just grand.

KEVIN: Could be a job 'ere for you George, now I'm moving up. I'll put in a word for you.

GEORGE (*delighted*): Well! Thank you.

JOYCE: Congratulations Kevin.

JOYCE *cuts the cake into pieces.*

GEORGE: When do you start?

KEVIN: I ain't sure, 'ave a look Wandsworth.

GEORGE *takes the letter, peers at it, but can't read it.*

GEORGE: I can't do long words yet.

He hands the letter back to KEVIN.

KEVIN (*to* JOYCE): You wouldn't like to run your eyes over this an' tell me when me money goes up would you?

JOYCE *takes the letter and reads it, she frowns then re-reads it.*

GEORGE: How much more will you get?

KEVIN: 'Bout twenty quid a week.

KEVIN *hands* GEORGE *and* THELMA *a slice of cake each.*

THELMA: I hope your hands are clean.

KEVIN: Course they are, I've just had 'em in running water.

THELMA *bites the cake.*

Down a drain.

He laughs and gives a piece of cake to the guy.

JOYCE: Kevin.

KEVIN: Yeah?

JOYCE: Oh Kevin.

KEVIN: What's up?

JOYCE: They're not renewing your contract.

KEVIN: What's that mean?

JOYCE: You've got the sack! I'm so sorry.

KEVIN: All right, joke over.

JOYCE: I wouldn't joke about a thing like that.

KEVIN (*snatching letter*): Where's it say?

JOYCE: There.

She points to the relevant paragraph.

KEVIN: *What's* it say?

JOYCE: It says, 'Your work has been found to be unsatisfactory, therefore the Education Committee reluctantly inform you that your contract is not to be renewed'.

GEORGE: Unsatisfactory! He's been here from morning till night. He's kept this place going.

JOYCE: I'm sorry.

KEVIN (*in shock*): The fucking bastards! I was the only one in our house that had a job. Now it's the whole bleedin' family on the dole. We'll hire a mini bus and go down there together, it'll be cheaper than the bus fare.

THELMA: He told me that his family were dead!

JOYCE: You've been given a fortnight's notice.

KEVIN: They can stuff that! I ain't working where I'm not wanted.

He takes his caretaker's coat off and throws it on the floor.

An' I ain't locking up tonight neither, nor going' round with the Harpic.

THELMA: You can't just leave the doors open. The public will take advantage.

KEVIN: I don't care, they can take what they like. It belongs to 'em. It comes out of the rates.

GEORGE: I'm sorry for your news Kevin.

KEVIN: I'm sorry for myself. It wasn't much of a job, but it were better than nothing.

THELMA: You brought it on yourself. You never cleaned behind the toilets properly and the wash basins were always filthy.

KEVIN: Fanks Thelma. (*Pause.*) I shall remember that when I'm standing in the queue waiting for some hatchet face to say, 'Put your cross here Mr Muldoon'.

JOYCE: If only you'd learn to read and write Kevin. It would help you get another job.

KEVIN (*shouts*): There are three and a half million can't get jobs. They ain't all illiterate.

GEORGE: But why don't you learn just for the sake of learning? There's some beautiful words in the language.

KEVIN: Yeah, like work and money.

JOYCE: But *why* don't you want to learn?

KEVIN: Look, I spent twelve years at school bein' taught. Seven of 'em with the same poxy book in front of me. I knew it off by heart.
Here we go, it's called. There's these two kids: one's called Janet and one's called John. They're both healthy lookin' kids, lucky bleeders an' all. They lived in this big posh house an' they was always going' for picnics an' swimmin' in the river. There's no

parents around in this book, though I have heard tell that they come on the scene in the next, but then I didn't get past the first did I? They're always tellin' each other to 'Look up!' 'Look down!', 'Look at the kitten!', 'Look at the bleedin' dog!', 'See my aeroplane!'. The most excitin' bit is when the dog runs off with the ball.

GEORGE: What happens next?

KEVIN: Nothing! It takes it into its kennel.

THELMA: We had Dick and Dora. They lived in a nice house as well. Their father carried a briefcase home every night. I put my hand up and asked the teacher what it was. She said 'It's a briefcase' in a horrible sort of way, but I hadn't seen one before. None of the men I knew carried them.

KEVIN: They don't want us to read! There ain't room for all of us is there?

JOYCE: That's absolute balls and you know it! The country needs a highly intelligent, literate workforce.

KEVIN: Why ain't it got one?

A long pause.

GEORGE: She needs prior notice on that question.

JOYCE: I'm on your side Kevin. Don't talk to me as if I were the enemy. I can't help being middle class. None of us can help our backgrounds. I vote Labour! And I do my best for the community. I don't have to come here every Wednesday, you know. My husband doesn't like it, and my friends think it's rather a joke.

KEVIN: They'll be laughing on the other side of their faces one day.

JOYCE: Come the revolution?

KEVIN: Yeah, come the revolution.

JOYCE: How novel! You'll be the only revolutionary not to have read Marx.

KEVIN: I've been told I've got street

validity. Apparently it counts for more these days.

JOYCE: So you'll be distributing leaflets that you can't read yourself will you?

KEVIN: Leaflets? Who's talkin' 'bout leaflets? I'll be passing out the ammunition.

JOYCE: Oh armed revolution?

KEVIN: Well we gotta have something. Your lot have got all the long words. And what have we got? This!

He pulls the 'gotcha' *edition of* The Sun *out of his pocket.*

JOYCE: That paper's years old.

KEVIN: I found it in the boiler house, I only kept it 'cos I can read the headline.

THELMA: What does it say?

KEVIN: Gotcha! The only headline I've ever been able to read an' you know why? Because they use it in the pissin' *Beano*!

He lashes out at the guy and knocks it on the floor.

GEORGE: Steady on! There's a lot of work gone into that.

KEVIN: You've been wasting your bleedin' time George. Didn't nobody tell you what happens to guys when they ain't needed anymore? They're put on a pile of rubbish and burnt!

He kicks it around the floor.

JOYCE: Stop it!

GEORGE: A lot of work went into that!

KEVIN: Why don't you do the country a favour George? Go on! Chuck yourself on the bonfire.

JOYCE: No more! Stop it!

JOYCE *slaps* KEVIN's *face.* KEVIN *slaps her back.*

GEORGE: You mustn't hit a woman!

KEVIN: It's an equal opportunity.

THELMA: He's gone mad, he wants certifying.

KEVIN: Do you want one an' all? Cos nothin' would give me more pleasure, you bleeding lackey.

THELMA: I'm not a lackey, I'm a nanny. Mrs Eirenstone got me from *The Lady*.

KEVIN: You're cheap labour ain't you? Gels like you are ten a penny. Another few months and Mrs Eirenstone will turf you out an' get somebody who can read an' write an' pay 'em the same pathetic money.

THELMA *flies at* KEVIN. KEVIN *gets his arm around her neck.*

GEORGE: That's enough now, you've said enough.

KEVIN: Tell 'em where you live George!

JOYCE: I don't want to know!

GEORGE: There's no need for that. You're rubbing salt in the wounds.

THELMA: He's strangling me.

JOYCE: Kevin please stop it. George don't just stand there.

KEVIN: He lives in the Wendy House, don't you George? In the bleeding Wendy House.

GEORGE *lunges at* KEVIN, *pulls* KEVIN's *arm from round* THELMA's *neck and wrestles him to the floor.*

JOYCE: Don't hurt him George.

GEORGE: He promised me he wouldn't say ought.

GEORGE *tightens his grip.*

JOYCE: George, please don't hurt him, he's only nineteen.

THELMA: People like him need hurting. They shouldn't be allowed to go around telling the truth. It's upsetting for all concerned.

KEVIN: Let me up George.

GEORGE: I'll let you up when you're calm.

KEVIN: Just tell me one thing

Mrs Charmer. Say if everybody could read good papers and good books how long would people stay on the Council Estates eh? And how long would it be before the dole and the Social Security were burning?

JOYCE: Let him up George.

GEORGE *gets off KEVIN.*

THELMA: That floor's filthy, it's no wonder he . . .

KEVIN *gets up,* JOYCE *and* GEORGE *dust him down.*

GEORGE (*shouting*): Shut up Thelma, don't start him off again.

KEVIN *runs out. Everyone is very shaken.*

THELMA: What was he talking about burning for? Is he going to set fire to the place?

GEORGE: It's just a young lad's talk. It's just hot air.

JOYCE (*picking up the guy*): Such a shame, it was a lovely guy.

GEORGE: Those posh papers you saved me helped a lot.

JOYCE: Could you follow the instructions in them?

GEORGE: No but they make better stuffing, there's more to 'em.

The lights go out. THELMA *screams. The pumpkins are glowing in the dark.*

JOYCE: Where are you Thelma?

THELMA: I'm here, I'm on my own.

GEORGE: Now don't you ladies panic. Everything's all right. I'm going to the door.

JOYCE: It's only a fuse gone Thelma.

THELMA: I can't be in the dark. She used to put me to bed in the dark, but it didn't do any good. If you can't read, then you can't read.

JOYCE: Open the door George.

GEORGE: I can't, it's locked. That silly bugger's gone and locked it.

GEORGE *gropes to the table and sits down.*

JOYCE: Put your arms round me Thelma.

THELMA *puts her arms around* JOYCE's *neck.*

THELMA: What's he doing it for?

JOYCE: He's very angry. The streets are full of them.

THELMA: It's not my fault he's lost his job is it? He shouldn't have touched me there.

Pause.

GEORGE: I don't know where I'm going to sleep tonight.

Pause.

JOYCE: If he was my son he'd be at university by now.

Sound of a key in the door.

GEORGE: That's him.

GEORGE *gropes towards the table where the women are sitting.* KEVIN *opens the door, he has a lit sparkler in his hand.*

THELMA (*screams*): He's going to burn us to death!

With the sparkler KEVIN *spells out* 'G'.

GEORGE: Guh.

JOYCE: G.

KEVIN *spells out* 'O'.

GEORGE: O.

JOYCE: O.

KEVIN *spells out* 'T'.

THELMA: Tuh.

JOYCE: T.

KEVIN *spells out* 'C'.

JOYCE: C.

Quicker now, KEVIN *spells out* 'H'.

GEORGE: H.

KEVIN *spells out* 'A'.

THELMA: A.

JOYCE: Gotcha!

KEVIN: Teach me to read!

WOMBERANG

Womberang was first presented at the Soho Poly Theatre Club, London, on 20 October 1979, with the following cast:

RITA	Joan Morrow
CLERK	Carolyn Pickles
DOLLY	Trudie Goodwin
MRS CONELLY	Fanny Carby
MRS LOVETT	Sheila Collins
JAMES	Kit Jackson
AUDREY	Fleure Chandler
LYNDA	Carolyn Pickles
MRS CORNWALLIS	Carolyn Pickles
MR RILEY	Kit Jackson

Directed by Sue Pomeroy
Designed by Dee Greenwood

A hospital outpatients' waiting room.
The afternoon gynaecological clinic is
in progress. A CLERK *at a desk faces*
padded benches, one of which has a pile
of tatty magazines stacked on it. On the
wall is a large ticking clock surrounded by
the usual notices. Blood-donor and anti-
smoking posters predominate. A large
sign simply says 'No Smoking'.
   A row of curtained cubicles stands
next to the DOCTOR'*s door. Two large*
free-standing ashtrays complete the
furnishings of this 'room'.
   A hospital smell would help the
atmosphere.
   MRS LOVETT *and* MRS CONELLY
sit on the front bench, AUDREY
LEMON *and* JAMES LEMON *sit on the*
bench behind them.
   There must be a long pause before:
RITA *and* DOLLY *enter. Everyone*
sitting looks up, stares. RITA *stares*
back, SITTERS *drop eyes.* RITA *and*
DOLLY *go to* CLERK'*s desk.* CLERK *is*
writing, ignoring the SITTERS. SITTERS
cough, shuffle and after thirty seconds
RITA *brings bell from large bag and rings*
it. There is an immediate result. The
CLERK *looks up and the* SITTERS *are*
riveted by the interruption to the sluggish
afternoon.

RITA: About bleedin' time! Don't you
   know it's very bad manners to ignore
   people? Writing can wait — you're
   only writing lists of names aren't you?

CLERK: You should have said!

RITA: You knew we were here!

(*To* SITTERS:) I ring it in shops now
   when they keep me waiting for
   nothing. Teaches them a lesson. They
   don't expect it.

CLERK: Have you got an appointment?

RITA: Yes, for half-past two, it is now
   two-fifteen by my watch, so in a
   quarter of an hour I shall be expecting
   to see Dr Riley.

CLERK: Well, we're running very late,
   you may have to wait a bit longer
   than half-past two.

RITA: I have a plane to catch at
   Heathrow Airport. It is crucial that my
   appointment is on time. You will have
   to tell Dr Riley to get his finger out,
   perhaps literally get his finger out.

RITA *and* DOLLY *laugh,* MRS
LOVETT, *a* SITTER, *sniggers.*

CLERK: Can I have your name?

RITA: If you like, but you might change
   your name when you hear it. It's Rita
   Onions, or if you prefer O-nions.

CLERK: Is that Miss or Mrs O-nions?

RITA: Divorced Rita O-nions, put what
   you like. Mr would be more suitable,
   short for mother.

CLERK: Would you take a seat?

RITA: Where to?

DOLLY *laughs.*

CLERK: Will you sit down?

RITA: Tidier that way aren't we?

DOLLY: C'mon, Reet, my feet are
   killin' me with walking round town.
   Let's sit down.

The two sit down on the front bench,
DOLLY *next to* MRS LOVETT.

RITA: Shall we have a fag?

DOLLY: No, it's no smokin', Reet!

RITA: Look, in a quarter of an hour
   I could find out I've got six months
   to live, if I don't need a fag now, when
   do I?

Both light up.

JAMES LEMON *is shocked.*

CLERK: I'm afraid there's no smoking.

RITA: Then why provide ashtrays?
   Bloody hypocrites!

CLERK: The smoke may be offensive to
   other patients!

JAMES LEMON *coughs.*

RITA: I'll ask them! (*To other*
   SITTERS:) This smoke bothering
   anyone?

No one reacts.

RITA (*stands, enunciates clearly*): I said, is this smoke bothering anyone? No? Good. Hands up who likes the smell of hospitals.

No one reacts.

RITA: The smoke wins by a clear (*To* CLERK:) if not devastating majority.

MRS CONELLY *gets up from the bench and goes to the desk.*

CONELLY (*in a loud whisper*): I'm very sorry, dear, but I've forgotten to bring a sample of water.

CLERK: Were you definitely told to bring one at your last consultation?

CONELLY: Yes, I'm sorry, but with all the worry . . .

CLERK: Well *I'm* sorry but the hospital can't be expected to provide containers, that's why you're told to bring them from home.

CONELLY: What shall I do then?

CLERK: I'd better make you another appointment. Will a fortnight today be all right, at the same time?

RITA (*standing*): No it will not.

(*To* CONELLY): Don't worry, love, I'll sort you out.

(*To all*): Who's got a bottle or jar — anything waterproof? They only need a drop of pee for Christ's sake.

DOLLY: Will this do, Reet? (*She holds up a tic-tac box.*)

RITA: No it will not, Dolly, this lady can't pee into a Tic-Tac box and neither could Olga Korvet . . . Somebody must have a bottle, come with me, duck, we'll find something.

RITA *takes* MRS CONELLY *out into the corridor.*

LOVETT (*to* DOLLY): You a friend of hers?

DOLLY (*proudly*): I'm her best friend.

LOVETT: Does she always carry on like that, or is she in a bad mood?

DOLLY: She's always the same nowadays, it's not a bad mood, it's more . . . now then, she did tell me, I've forgotten the word . . . it's quite a long one, not one you use every day . . . one of those.

LOVETT: Paranoia?

DOLLY: No, it doesn't begin with a P, although that's the type of word. Are you educated then?

LOVETT: Not properly, who is? No, I used to clean for a doctor. He used to let me take some of his books home to read. Then one of my neighbours went funny during the change — you know. She thought everyone was talkin' about her, saying her house smelt. I looked it up and it was called paranoia, it sort of stuck in my mind. (*Pause.*) Between you and me, her house did smell.

DOLLY: I wish I could remember that word, still, Reet will be back soon, she'll tell you.

LOVETT: It's quiet in here again without her. She's like a one-woman show.

DOLLY: Yes, she's a case isn't she? You wouldn't have known her last year. Her husband walked all over her, got so bad she wouldn't go out of the house, kids did all the shopping, she sat by the fire watching telly all day, then cleaned the house over and over when the kids were in bed. Not normal is it?

LOVETT *shakes her head.*

Anyway, her doctor sent her to the Towers, got an order from the court, she wouldn't go voluntary, wouldn't leave the kids. But oh, you should have seen her at the end, like a wild woman she was. *I* had to go in and feed the kids, do the washing and all that. She sat in a chair filthy, watching the telly, didn't speak a word to nobody, then one night one of the kids burnt themselves on the stove

making some toast. Reet never moved, didn't turn her head. They took the kids away that night, in care they call it.
I told them I'd have them, but they said we was already overcrowded anyway. Reet goes in the Towers like a zombie and comes out like you've seen her today.

LOVETT: Did she have the electric shock?

DOLLY: Yes, but it wasn't that, it was the therapy group. Therapy, that's where they all sit around and tell everyone in the group what they really think, really think!
Like say if someone's got dirty teeth, they tell them . . .

The SITTERS *all become teeth-conscious.*

. . . I think you should clean your teeth. Awful isn't it? Or if they've got a bogy in their nose . . . you tell them, you tell them all about when you were a kid. If your husband drives you mad when he's eating. Things you wouldn't normally tell nobody. Reet was quiet at first, didn't talk much, then somebody said her roots needed doing, she's not a natural blonde — but don't say anything. Well Reet went wild, called him everything from a pig to a cow. After that she's been the same as you saw her today, speaks her mind, does things instead of sitting quiet.

LOVETT: She's a bit much though, isn't she? Doesn't she show you up?

DOLLY: Yes she does, but she's a good friend to me. F'rinstance, my baker's been fiddling me for years. You know what they do, charge you for cakes you haven't had, leave bread you haven't ordered, it soon mounts up.

MRS LOVETT *and* AUDREY LEMON *nod.*

LOVETT: I'd have told him first time it happened, you're daft to have put up with it.

DOLLY: Some can, some can't. I could never pluck up the courage. Reet made me tell him. She stood behind the door.
I said, 'I shan't want no more bread.' He said, 'When, this week?' 'No, never,' I says and Reet shot from behind the door and says, 'And she won't be paying this week's bill neither, take it out of what you've fiddled from her over the years.'
Well he never said a word, just got into his van and drove off. Oh, it was so lovely not having him call every day, but I did feel a bit sorry for him.

LOVETT: Serves the bugger right. (*She laughs.*) Who was it, Co-op?

DOLLY: Yes, how did you know? (*All the* WOMEN *laugh.*)

LOVETT: What's she here for then?

DOLLY (*dropping her voice*): She's not been right down below.

LOVETT: Waterworks?

DOLLY: Well near there, very near.

LOVETT: Baby trouble?

DOLLY: Not exactly baby trouble in that area.

LOVETT: Dropped has it?

DOLLY: Has what dropped?

LOVETT: Her womb!

DOLLY: I think it's more stuck than dropped.

LOVETT: Stuck eh! Never heard of that. I'm here for a drop. I'm expecting to have it all took away. Should have happened years ago. I suffered in silence for years, didn't think the family could spare me for going into hospital.
Now I don't care if the selfish sods starve while I'm in, do 'em all good to do their own washing as well. If I don't have the operation soon, I'll cut my throat, that's how I feel.

RITA *enters.*

RITA: Well, in this age of medical technology, an old age pensioner is peeing into a Coca-Cola bottle using a *Beano* comic as a funnel. Look good in the *Standard* wouldn't it, dear? (*She glares at the* CLERK.) I can see the results of the test now: 'Mrs Conelly is suffering from Desperate Dan-itis and Beryl the Peril syndrome.'

RITA, DOLLY, LOVETT *and* AUDREY *laugh.* JAMES *silences* AUDREY.

DOLLY: I was telling this lady about you, Reet, since your therapy.

RITA: Oh yes? She'll be thinking I'm a loony, Dolly, all I do is speak my mind and tell the truth. It's good for you, that's what therapy means, good for you. I bet most of us here are only imagining things wrong with us. If we had a talk I bet we'd walk out of here blooming with health.

CLERK: Mrs Lovett, would you undress and go and sit in the cubicle on the right please, Mr Riley won't keep you long.

MRS LOVETT *stands.*

RITA: Yes he will keep her long! He's just got his tea and bisuits, and he's lit up one of them small cigars. I just saw him through the crack in the door. Take your time Mrs Lovett, and another thing, don't put your feet in them stirrup things, let them learn to look at our faces first, instead of our bums. It's undignified for all concerned.

CLERK: Mrs O-nions, I must ask you not to interfere with medical matters, you are not qualified to give advice to these ladies.

RITA: You're not qualified to give advice to me, you sweet little school leaver, making an old age pensioner piss into a Coca-Cola bottle!

MRS CONELLY *enters holding Coca-Cola bottle half full of pee.*

CONELLY: Here it is, dear, I couldn't manage much, is there enough?

RITA: You can have some of mine if you like, that'll baffle the sods.

CLERK: That's enough! Now sit down and shut up. You're getting all of this free you know! You shouldn't mock it, it's sacrilege! It's bad enough working with disgusting, ill people all day, without having them being rude to me as well. I've had enough. I'm off.
I shall have to report you, Mrs O-nions.

The CLERK *exits.*

DOLLY: Now you've done it, Reet.

RITA: She's not suited to the job is she? One day she might have a difficult patient to deal with, I'm only giving her a bit of training. Anyway, now she's gone, let's talk, all of us. Let's change the benches round so we can see each other properly. Light your fags up if you want to, Riley's in there smoking his cigar.

The WOMEN *change the benches around,* JAMES *and* AUDREY *remain seated, they are pulled around by the other* WOMEN.

Right, are we all comfy? Someone has to start the ball rolling . . . or the womb dropping. (*She laughs.*) *Remember?* That lady's fat isn't she, Mummy? Slap. (RITA *slaps her wrist.*) Uncle Ted, your ears stick out. (*She slaps herself.*) I expect you've done it to your own kids, teach them to tell the truth, then smack 'em round the ear'ole if they do.
Right, shall I start?

There are wary nods from DOLLY, LOVETT *and* CONELLY.

Mrs Conelly, dear, did you know your corsets show right through your dress? If I were you I'd wear a looser dress or throw the bloody corset away.

CONELLY: But I've always worn it. It keeps me in, it keeps me back straight. I shouldn't feel dressed without it.

RITA: Group, what does she look like in it?

Silence.

RITA: Come on, the truth now!

ALL WOMEN EXCEPT AUDREY: Take it off. Awful. You can see every whalebone.

RITA: Go on, take it off, Mrs Conelly. Let it all hang out.

CONELLY: I'll think about it, promise. I'll give it some thought.

RITA: Good. Right, who's next?

The GROUP *becomes uncomfortable.*

RITA (*to* JAMES): Who are you? Not waiting to see the gynaecologist are you? Don't want a sex change?

JAMES *is reading* Watchtower.

JAMES: I'm accompanying my wife, and I'd rather you didn't include either of us in your game.

RITA: Oh. It isn't a game, duck, it's serious. Go on, let yourself go. Your as wound up as a milkman's alarm clock. Anyway perhaps your wife does want to take part?

AUDREY *shakes her head after looking at* JAMES.

RITA: Don't ask him! Do you want to take part?

AUDREY *shakes her head.*

RITA: Are you mute, dear? Are you lip-reading? If so I will speak very clearly. One – more – time – do – you – want – to – take – part – question – mark.

AUDREY (*clearing her throat*): I can speak. (*She looks at* JAMES.) But if my husband doesn't want me to take part, then I won't.

JAMES *pats* AUDREY'*s arm.*

RITA: Do my ears deceive me? You've just put Women's Liberation back ten years. I bet Christabel . . . wotsit is whirling in her grave.

LOVETT: Pankhurst. Christabel Pankhurst.

RITA: Thanks, dear.

(*To* AUDREY): Now you can tell me what your name is, can't you, or will your hubby mind?

JAMES *whispers to* AUDREY.

AUDREY: It's Mrs Audrey Lemon.

RITA: We make a right pair, don't we? Onions and Lemons. Like the kid's song:

(*She sings*.) Onions and Lemons.

LOVETT: Oranges! (*She gets no response*.) It's oranges (*To herself*.)

AUDREY *laughs.*
JAMES *stands.*

JAMES: I forbid you to speak another word to my wife, she leads a very sheltered life, she has an extremely nervous disposition.

DOLLY: I get nerves. (*She sees* RITA'*s glance*.) Now . . . and again. (*Her voice fades*.)

RITA: Audrey, does he always speak to you like this?

AUDREY: Mm. I suppose he does.

RITA: Today will be the last day, Audrey, you have my word.

AUDREY: It doesn't bother me, not really.

RITA: It bothers me, dear.

JAMES: Audrey needs a firm hand, she *can* be headstrong.

RITA: By the look of her she needs a firm something. Why are you here, Audrey, something wrong?

JAMES: Audrey!

RITA: Go on, love.

AUDREY: We've been married five years and . . .

JAMES: Audrey!

AUDREY: James has been waiting for

kiddies to come along and they haven't, so I've got to have some tests —

JAMES: Audrey! I won't tell you again, you will not discuss our private life with this woman!

AUDREY *looks at* RITA *who gives her an encouraging gesture.*

AUDREY: James, Mrs Onions is quite right, I ought to be allowed to speak if I want to.

JAMES: I'm warning you, Audrey, open your mouth one more time and I'm off. You can face the doctor on your own.

AUDREY: Please, James, it can't do any harm.

JAMES: Have you gone mad? I've just told you to keep your mouth shut.

AUDREY: Well I won't!

JAMES: Shut it!

AUDREY: No!

JAMES: Shut your mouth!

AUDREY: Piss off!

JAMES: Audrey, you swore.

AUDREY: I might swear again.

JAMES: Think of your mother.

AUDREY: Bugger!

JAMES: Audrey!

AUDREY: I might say the really bad word!

JAMES: God help you, Audrey.

AUDREY: You need his help more than I do!

JAMES: I'll have to report you to the brethren.

AUDREY: You can tell them to piss off too. I'm sick of seeing their miserable faces, no smoking, no drinking, no Christmas, not even a blood transfusion.

JAMES: You've lost your faith!

AUDREY: I've never had it, James.

Every week trudging around preaching the message no one wants to hear. You've seen their faces change when they realise who we are, and James, I don't believe we'll be saved at Armageddon, if it ever comes we'll die like all the rest.

JAMES: You're condemned to everlasting death now, you realise that don't you? You're past saving now, I'll have to leave . . . you're unclean.

(*To* RITA:) You're an agent of the Devil with your bleached hair and cigarettes.

RITA: I'm a natural blonde! I'll show you my armpits if you like.

JAMES *rushes out.*

DOLLY: Oh God! You've really done it now, Reet.

RITA: Me! What did I do? She did it all herself. Good girl! Been waiting long to tell him all that?

AUDREY: Five years!

RITA: Feel better now?

AUDREY: Much better.

LOVETT: He looked like a right miserable sod to me, you're well rid of him. You a Jehovah's Witness then?

AUDREY: I was, until a few moments ago. I hope he never comes back, never, if he goes home today, I shall go and get a job. Start again.

LOVETT: Well good luck to you, gal, I say.

RITA: What about the doctor? Will you still see him?

AUDREY: There's no point. There's nothing wrong with me. It's just that some men don't know about certain things.

RITA: What kind of certain things?

AUDREY: Well, intimate things . . .

LOVETT: She means sex.

CONELLY: Some men don't know how to go on, my husband was a bit slow coming forward. We had to practise quite a lot.

RITA: Are you telling me your husband's brought you down here for a check up and really it's him who doesn't know how to go on?

AUDREY: Yes, he wasn't doing it right.

RITA: How was he doing it?

DOLLY: Reet!

RITA: Is he one of them perverts?

DOLLY: Reet!

AUDREY: No. Nothing like that. It's just that instead of putting it in here (*She indicates her groin.*) he was putting it there. (*She indicates her navel.*)

RITA: What! In your belly button?

AUDREY *nods.*

RITA: Not so much making love as a bleeding naval exercise! Why didn't you tell him?

AUDREY: I just couldn't, he wouldn't allow any talk about sex, he'd walk out of the room if I tried to talk. I never once saw him undressed — and he never saw me. He'd close his eyes. It's his mother's fault, she brought him up to think that women were dirty. Perhaps she told him babies were born out of your tummy button.

LOVETT: He must have been going around with his eyes and ears shut for years. Like them Japanese that think the war's still on.

RITA: It's sad really, just think what he's missing.

LOVETT: I shouldn't miss it. I've had no rockets firing or bells ringing for me. It's a quick grope when the club shuts on Sunday afternoon. He's stinking of beer and I've got an Oxo cube in me hand and I'm lying there smelling me meat burning in the oven.

DOLLY: I'm all right there, I've got one of those pre-timers, my meat switches itself off.

RITA: All right! All right! Before we get bogged down with self-cleaning ovens and bloody washing-machines, let's get back to Audrey.
So you think it's all over do you, love? Starting out on your own? Join the club, it can be done, can't it Dolly? We're both on our own, we have a good laugh. No shirts to wash and iron, none of them big slimy handkerchiefs to wash, no dinner to be on the table at dead on six.

DOLLY: I sometimes miss my John, late at night, when Reet's gone home. The kids miss him, they're always asking when he's coming home. I have to keep on thinking up new excuses. At the moment he's supposed to be drilling for oil in Bahrain.

RITA: That's a laugh, couldn't fill his lighter without spilling it all over the place.

LOVETT: If he's gone for good, you should tell the kids, it's not fair to keep them hoping.

RITA: Dolly thinks he will come back, don't you, Dolly? She thinks he'll leave his posh flat and his page-three bird to come back to his council house, three screaming kids and Racquel Welch here.

DOLLY: Honestly, Reet, sometimes you can be so cruel.

DOLLY *is almost in tears.*

RITA: I'm cruel to be kind, Dolly, you know that.

AUDREY: I think I'll go now, I've got a lot to do. I'm that excited, it's like being born again! I can please myself, do as I like. I can't wait to start.

GROUP: Good luck! Mind how you go!

AUDREY *gathers her bags, smiles at the door, waves and leaves.*

AUDREY: Bye! Bye!

RITA: I'll give her six months before she finds a bloke from the Divine Light Mission or one of them Moonies. She's a natural victim that one.

CONELLY: She seemed a really nice girl.

RITA: They always are.

LOVETT: Anyway, who's next?

RITA *sighs – a deep sigh of satisfaction, stretches her body on the seat and sits with her hands behind her head, the epitome of relaxation.*

RITA: You don't do it like that, there has to be a general discussion, then it gets more personal. Let's talk about politics.

GROUP: Oh no. I don't know anything . . .

RITA: All right then, we won't talk about politics, we'll talk about Mrs Thatcher.

DOLLY: Oh she dresses lovely! And her hair always looks nice as well, just as if she's stepped out of the hairdresser's.

RITA: That's because she has, Dolly. But do you think she's a good Prime Minister?

CONELLY: Well I've noticed that her voice has got deeper since she started, it must be all that talking.

RITA: That's only on the telly and for speeches, I'll bet she talks different at home.

She gives a Thatcher impression.

Denis! Denis! Come and empty this filthy ashtray.

All the WOMEN *laugh.*

LOVETT: I've got nothing to thank her for. The night my husband came home and told me that he'd been laid-off I could have strangled her.
He'd been crying on his way home, he'd been there twenty years. All his mates were there. He still gets up at the same time, sometimes he forgets and puts his boot on. It's a habit you see, going to work.

RITA: What makes me laugh is how nobody admits to voting for her.

DOLLY (*blushing*): Did you read in *Woman* that Mrs Thatcher has never asked her husband about his first wife?

LOVETT: Oh, I didn't know he'd been married before.

RITA: You mean they don't talk about his first wife?

DOLLY: No, they've never talked about her, not once!

LOVETT: Not natural is it? I should have wanted all the details, what she liked for breakfast, did she have her own teeth, everything.

RITA: Politicians are not normal though are they? I spoke to one once at a Christmas Bazaar. He said, 'Do you live round here?' I said, 'Yes.' He said, 'How lovely. How lovely!' I said, 'It's not lovely, it's where they put all the bad tenants.' But his eyes glazed over and he walked off.

CONELLY: I saw William Whitelaw once when he came to our Community Centre. He's got bad teeth.

RITA: What did he say?

CONELLY: He didn't say anything, he made a speech.

LOVETT: I saw Len Fairclough when he opened Wilkinson's Hardware. He's shorter than you think. Looks as if he needs to eat more greens.

LYNDA *enters clutching her belly.*

LYNDA (*startled*): Oh! Am I in the right place?

RITA: Yes, and at the right time by the look of you. When's it due?

LYNDA: On the twenty-ninth. I'm overdue.

LOVETT: It won't be long, it's dropped.

LYNDA: Has it?

LOVETT: You've got a boy in there. It's all at the front. I've never been wrong yet. You could bet a million pounds on it. I hope you want a boy because that's what you've got — a boy.

LYNDA: I don't mind what it is . . .

ALL: As long as it's all right.

LYNDA: I think they're going to induce me.

RITA: Oh they will. Babies aren't allowed to be born late nowadays.

LOVETT: Or at weekends.

DOLLY: Or late at night.

CONELLY: Except on Christmas Eve.

RITA: Or New Year's Day, so they can get in the paper. What's your name, love?

LYNDA: Lynda, with a Y.

DOLLY: I was induced with one of mine. (*She adds in a comforting manner.*) But don't worry, it's all right.

RITA: Don't tell bloody lies, Dolly! You told me it was a nightmare, you screamed your bloody head off.

DOLLY: Reet!

RITA: I won't take part in this conspiracy, Dolly. True, some women have 'em like shelling peas, but for some it's painful, even agonising. Scream your head off, love, that way they fill you so full of Pethidene you won't care if they drive a steamroller over you.

LYNDA: Oh, it won't be like that for me, I've been to relaxation classes, there's no need for it to be painful, after all it's a natural process.

RITA: So is toothache a natural process.

LYNDA: But there's no need to have a toothache if you take care of your teeth and go to the dentist regularly.

RITA: And you do?

LYNDA: Of course.

RITA: I bet you bake your own bread, don't you? Brown bread with all them nasty bits in it. Am I right?

LYNDA: Yes, how did you know?

RITA: I saw the *Guardian* in your bag. My social worker's wife reads the *Guardian*. She looks a bit like you. She bakes her own bread. I know because when he gets round my house all them nasty bits are stuck between his teeth.

LYNDA: The whole grain.

RITA: He goes on at me to try it but quite honestly I think you must be a bit mental to go to all that trouble when you can nip out and buy a sliced loaf.

CONELLY: I think she's right, dear. I remember *having* to bake the bread. I'd be there all day mixing, kneading, keeping it out of the draughts. Then watching the oven, and nine times out of ten it turned out wrong.

Everyone laughs.

LOVETT: Like the dolly tub and the washing. Some used to swear that it got your sheets whiter than the machines. So what? I say, bung it in the machine and have the time to yourself, I say.

RITA: I bet you're on a lot of committees, aren't you? Preserving things?

LYNDA: Not many. Mostly jam now. (*She gives a little laugh.*)

RITA: You look healthy. I bet you take your iron tablets every day.

LYNDA: Yes.

RITA: Grow your own vegetables?

LYNDA: Yes.

RITA: You make your own clothes too by the look of them, don't you?

LYNDA: Yes.

RITA: And shop at Sainsbury's?

DOLLY: *You* shop at Sainsbury's, Reet!

RITA: But I don't buy yogurt, Dolly!

LYNDA: Nor do I. I make my own.

RITA: See! See! I knew it! She would wouldn't she? I'll bet your library books are never overdue. What are you calling the baby?

LYNDA: If it's a girl, Florrie.

The WOMEN *giggle.*

LYNDA: If it's a boy, Hereward.

The WOMEN *laugh.*

RITA: Hereward! Poor little sod!

LYNDA: They are both very old English names.

LOVETT: I had a dog called Florrie, she got distemper from the ferrets. We had to have her put down.

RITA: When he gets to school, they'll kill Hereward, have you thought about that?

LYNDA: Our child will be taught to tolerate the ignorance of others.

RITA: Teach him boxing at the same time then, do him more good.

LYNDA *gasps and clutches her belly.*

RITA: Are you all right, love?

DOLLY: She looks awful!

LYNDA: I feel as if I've wet myself.

RITA: Is it a lot?

LYNDA: It's still coming! I can't stop it!

LYNDA *grows very very slowly hysterical. She makes no loud sounds but her breathing attempts a pattern, then fails.*

RITA: You don't need your fancy breathing yet, it's only a show.

RITA: You're not in proper labour yet.

DOLLY: It's her waters broken, Reet.

LYNDA (*moans*): Help me! Help me!

She falls to the floor and rolls around.

DOLLY: Undo her bra!

RITA: Shut up, Dolly!

LOVETT: We'd better fetch a nurse.

RITA: She'll have to calm down first, they'll think she's a loony. Lynda, calm down and shut up, or I'll smack you round the chops.

LYNDA *carries on.*

Lynda, I'll give you three, then I'll smack you. One – two – three.

RITA *smacks* LYNDA's *face; there is instant silence.*

Dolly, go and fetch a wheelchair, I'll take her up to maternity. All right now, love? Good girl.

DOLLY *leaves.*

LYNDA: I'm so sorry. It took me by surprise. I'm so frightened though. Is it true it's so painful?

RITA: Yes it's true. But you'll have a baby at the end of it. *I* think it's worth it.

CONELLY: I've had two boys and I hardly felt a thing, you might be like me.

LYNDA: Oh yes, I might! Thank you.

DOLLY *returns pushing a wheelchair.*

DOLLY: I got it from the X-ray department next door.

RITA: Right, let's have you in it, Lynda.

The WOMEN *help* LYNDA *into the wheelchair.*

CONELLY: You'll be all right, my love. I shall be thinking of you.

LYNDA: Thank you.

RITA: Comfy?

LYNDA *nods.*

RITA: Right, we're off.

GROUP: Good luck! Best of luck!

RITA *wheels* LYNDA *out.*

LOVETT: Well what a to-do! And all over the waters breaking! She looked such a nice girl as well. Nicely spoken too.

CONELLY: Won't be long before Florrie or Hereward's here then, will it?

All the WOMEN *laugh.*

DOLLY: Anyone want a drink? I don't usually in the day but it's my birthday tomorrow.

LOVETT: I'll have one, what is it, gin?

DOLLY *hands over half a bottle of gin.*

CONELLY: Not for me thanks, gin goes straight to my head. Last time I had gin I made a fool of myself. I did a dance in my corsets, using me teeth as castanets. It was five years ago at Christmas, at our Edna's party. I'd only had a couple of glasses. So I shan't, thank you anyway.

LOVETT: Go on, have one. A swig won't hurt you.

DOLLY: Go on, keep us company.

CONELLY: Oh all right, just a small one though, have we got a glass?

LOVETT: Just swig it out of the bottle, nobody's looking. Go on.

CONELLY *swigs heavily.*

LOVETT: Hey! Steady on! You've still to see the doctor remember. You can't go in there *stinking* of gin.

CONELLY: It wouldn't matter if I didn't go in, I only come to hear his voice, he's got such a lovely voice, so gentle and kind. Is he Scots?

LOVETT: No he's Irish, from Dublin. I asked him once. His first name is Declan. I steamed a letter open he'd written to my doctor, it was signed 'yours Declan'.

RITA *enters.*

RITA: I see Dolly's at the gin again.

DOLLY (*hurriedly*): How is she, Reet?

RITA: I took her straight up to the Labour ward in the lift. They weren't very pleased. It's probably thrown their whole schedule out, having a baby born in its own time. What you been talking about then?

CONELLY: I was just saying I only come to hear Dr Riley's voice. I don't need to come, I know what's wrong with me.

LOVETT: What's wrong then, duck?

CONELLY: It's not very nice to talk about it, people don't like it. You won't.

LOVETT: You can tell us anything, we won't mind.

CONELLY: All right.

Pause.

RITA: Go on, love.

CONELLY: I've got carcinoma of the womb.

DOLLY: Oh, it sounds awful. What is it?

RITA: It's cancer by a posh name. But it's cancer. (*Slight pause.*) Can they do anything? Are you having treatment?

CONELLY: I've had an operation and I've had treatment, but when my hair started falling out I stopped it. I'm not dying bald. I've always had nice hair. I take tablets for the pain and when it gets too bad to bear I shall take the lot and finish myself off. I come to see Dr Riley to find out how long I've got.

RITA: Does he tell you?

CONELLY: As near as he can.

RITA: How long have you got then?

CONELLY: I should have been dead last week, according to him.

She indicates RILEY*'s door. There is a slight pause, then they all laugh.*

CONELLY: Let's have another drink, Rita do you want one? You've not had one yet.

RITA: Yes, I'll have one. (*She takes a swig.*) Here's to you, love. I hope you enjoy what time you've got left. What's your name?

CONELLY: Mrs Conelly.

RITA: Not your *husband*'s name, your name.

CONELLY: It's Evelyn.

GROUP: Nice, pretty name.

RITA: I'd like to propose a toast to Evelyn. Let's hope the rest of your life is happy.

RITA *drinks and passes the bottle round.*

CONELLY: Thank you everyone. I wish I could say I've had a happy life. (*She shows no self-pity – there is more surprise.*) But I can't think of anything really . . . apart from the war, but then everyone was happy in the war. It was nice when the boys were small and I'll miss not seeing my grandchildren grow up but that's all. Makes you wonder why you're put on this earth.

DOLLY: *I've* often wondered that, have you, Reet?

RITA: We're here to provide the next generation, that's all.

LOVETT: There must be more to it than that!

CONELLY: Well, if it's what Rita says about the next generation, I've done that. We lived in a rough area but my boys grew up nice – never any trouble with the police. They've both got good jobs as well, one's got his own office.

RITA: There you are then, you've done your bit. More than I have. My kids are in care, but I'm getting them out as soon as I'm properly discharged from the Towers. I see 'em three times a week, don't I, Dolly? Every time I see them they ask, 'Can we come home today, Mum?'

Pause.

CONELLY: Oh it's so hot in here, you know, I think I will take these corsets off. (*She giggles.*) That gin's gone straight to my head. I've had nothing to eat today. (*She stands.*) These corsets have been a torment to me all my life. I'll take them off, I'll go into one of the cubicles. If Dr Riley wants me, tell him I shan't bother. Besides I've had too much to drink,

I shouldn't keep a straight face.

Everyone laughs.

CONELLY *goes into a cubicle.*

RITA: Do you want some help?

CONELLY: Can you undo the laces at the back? It'll save me the struggling?

RITA: Come out here then, there's not much room in there.

CONELLY: What if somebody comes?

RITA: They can't lock you up for taking your corsets off. (*Undressing* CONELLY.) This is a nice dress.

CONELLY: I got it from a rummage sale at Hampstead. It's worth the extra bus fare – everything is so clean.

RITA: We get our stuff from War on Want, don't we Dolly?

DOLLY: Not everything, not underwear.

RITA *has to help* CONELLY *off with her cardigan, dress, long petticoat, until she is standing in her hat, corsets and shoes.*

LOVETT: Christ! It's terrible. How do you get it on and off?

CONELLY: I'm used to it, it doesn't take long.

RITA (*laughing*): What *do* you look like?

CONELLY: I don't care, I once did a dance in me corsets at a party, I'd had a few drinks, I was telling Dolly and Mrs Lovett just now.

LOVETT: I wish I'd seen that.

RITA: Show us your dance, do it now.

DOLLY: No Reet, not here, not in a hospital.

LOVETT: Why not? Go on, do it, Evelyn. We'll clap, won't we?

RITA: Go on, Evelyn, it's all yours.

CONELLY: I have to take my teeth out first.

The WOMEN *are laughing and excited.*

CONELLY (*turns back, takes out her teeth*): Right give me some room!

She sings 'Viva Espana', dances around the room, climbs with help on to a bench, dances and clacks her false teeth.

Come on, join in.

The WOMEN *join in, dancing flamenco-style.*

JAMES LEMON *and a woman,* MRS CORNWALLIS, *who is the* ASSISTANT HOSPITAL ADMINISTRATOR *enter, and stand and stare at the scene in front of them.*

JAMES (*pointing to* RITA): That's her!

The WOMEN *stop dancing.* CONELLY *remains standing on the bench.*

MRS CORNWALLIS: You are Mrs Rita O-nions?

RITA: Rita Onions, yes.

MRS CORNWALLIS: I am the Assistant Hospital Administrator. I have received two complaints about your conduct in this waiting room. You are alleged to have smoked, used bad language, changed the furniture around, abused patients and interfered in medical matters and now I see you're drinking gin! Do you know it smells like a public bar in here?

RITA: No, I use the lounge myself.

JAMES: Has my wife seen the doctor yet?

RITA, LOVETT *and* DOLLY *laugh.*

RITA: No, she didn't need to. It's you that needs to, he'll tell you the correct position for sexual intercourse.

JAMES: Stop it! Tell her to stop it! (*He puts his hands over his ears.*)

MRS CORNWALLIS: Mr Lemon, you're overwrought. Go to my office. You take the lift to the basement, then once out of the lift it's the second corridor on the left, carry straight down until you see a door marked

mortuary. My office is opposite. Go in and make yourself a cup of tea. The teabags are in the second drawer down in my deak. The key to the drawer is on the back of the door marked with a two. Please lock the drawer and replace the key when you have finished your tea. Here's the key to the office.

JAMES *leaves.*

MRS CORNWALLIS: Mrs O-nions, please leave now!

RITA: I'll go when I've seen Dr Riley.

MRS CORNWALLIS: It's *Mr* Riley, he is a consultant.

RITA: Marvellous isn't it, they sweat for seven years to get the Dr in front of their names, then sweat again for God knows how long to get it taken off.

MRS CORNWALLIS: I'm a very busy person Mrs Onions. If you will leave now, I will make you another appointment for next week.

DOLLY *stands.*

RITA: When I've seen the doctor. Sit down, Dolly, we're not going anywhere!

DOLLY *sits.*

MRS CORNWALLIS: Why is this lady in her underwear?

RITA: She was changing to see the doctor.

MRS CORNWALLIS: Why has she got her teeth in her hand?

RITA: Ask her, she's not deaf and dumb.

CONELLY *tries to reply, but breaks into laughter.* LOVETT, RITA *and* DOLLY *join in.*

She thought she might have to have an emergency operation. (*She laughs.*) She should have been dead last week.

There is a great gust of laughter, from RITA, DOLLY, LOVETT *and* CONELLY *who all clutch each other.*

MRS CORNWALLIS: How sick! All four

of you are drunk. You can come back next week at the same time, I'll make sure we have extra staff to cope. Leave now before I call the police.

RITA *lights a fag.*

MRS CORNWALLIS: The notice! (*She points to the No Smoking sign.*)

RITA: The ashtray! (*She points to the ashtray.*)

There is a pause – RITA *and the* ASSISTANT HOSPITAL ADMINISTRATOR *eye each other up for five seconds.*

MRS CORNWALLIS (*to* MRS CONELLY): For goodness' sake, woman, get dressed! Go into a cubicle and get out of my sight, an old woman like you! You should be ashamed! What if your family found out? Perhaps they ought to know what you get up to.

MRS CONELLY *goes into a cubicle.*

RITA: You carry on talking like that and I'll break your ugly, fat neck.

MRS CORNWALLIS: You're obviously an unstable personality. I won't allow you to roam this hospital at will. You have threatened *me* with violence, *me!* I trained in the Towers, I recognise an unstable personality when I see one.

DOLLY: No! She's better now, they got her better, she –

RITA: Dolly, shut it!

MRS CORNWALLIS: You've been in the Towers?

RITA: Yes.

MRS CORNWALLIS: Were you a voluntary patient?

RITA: I'm not answering any more questions. I'll sit here and wait to see the doctor.

MRS CORNWALLIS: I'm going to ring the Towers. I'll find out about you Mrs Onions, and they'll find out just how you've been conducting yourself

since your release. They may want you back for an assessment. Who's your consultant at the Towers?

RITA *doesn't reply.*

MRS CORNWALLIS: I'll find out quickly enough, you may as well tell me.

RITA: I can't pronounce it, it's full of k's and z's, he's Polish. He's barmy as well, he washes his hands the whole time he's talking to the patients. He's frightened their madness will contaminate him. He thinks it's catching.

MRS CORNWALLIS: It's probably Dr Zedeweski you're refering to. Like all brilliant men he has his own harmless eccentricities.

RITA: He's just plain barmy, everyone knows it, they've been trying to get rid of him for years. And there he still is, in charge of all those unhappy people. Just wait until I'm properly discharged, I'll get rid of the mad old bugger.

MRS CORNWALLIS: So you're not properly discharged?

RITA: Community care they call it. I'm supposed to slot back into society without a ripple. I'm in the charge of a social worker. He's a nice bloke, means well, but his marriage is breaking up, so he's a bit preoccupied. He's having an affair with a lady policeman. He's told me all about it. *He* wanted *my* advice, should he leave his wife and kids? So who's looking after who?

MRS CORNWALLIS (*patronising*): Come with me to my office, Mrs O-nions. It's quite cosy with its rubber plants and electric coal fire. I'll make you a nice cup of tea.

RITA: No thank you, by the time you've unlocked the teabags I shouldn't be thirsty.

MRS CORNWALLIS: You're obviously overwrought, your libido isn't quite

ticking over at the right speed is it? I completely understand. The stresses and strains of the urban environment take their toll on us all. Escalating VAT . . .

LOVETT: Milk's going up. It's the Common Market.

All turn to MRS LOVETT, *all turn back.*

MRS CORNWALLIS: After the last porters' strike I was a mere shell of my former self. How much easier life was when we were all in the caves. (*She puts an arm around* RITA'*s shoulder.*)

RITA: Please take your arm off my shoulders.

MRS CORNWALLIS: A little support, that's all, dearie.

RITA: My bra gives me all the support I want. Take your bleedin' arm off my shoulders!

The ASSISTANT HOSPITAL ADMINISTRATOR *grabs* RITA'*s wrist. They struggle.*

CONELLY: Leave her alone, it's a few years since I smacked anyone round the ear'ole, but I haven't forgotten how it's done.

LOVETT: I'll join in an' all, let go of her!

MRS CORNWALLIS: This woman is potentially dangerous, it's more than my job's worth to let her loose again in this hospital.

DOLLY (*to* MRS CORNWALLIS): I shouldn't make her mad, she's been to night school for Kung Fu, she's ever so good.

RITA *struggles free and goes into Kung Fu attitude.*

RITA: I can see the headlines in the *Standard* now, four inches high — 'Old Age Pensioner Degraded, Shock Birth in Waiting Room'. By the time the *Sun* gets hold of it it'll be 'Old Age Pensioner Gives Birth in a Bottle'.

DOLLY: But that wouldn't be true, Reet!

RITA: That doesn't matter in newspapers, honestly sometimes you're as thick as two short planks!

MRS CORNWALLIS: Violence is the last resort of the ignorant, Mrs O-nions. I will not be intimidated by *it* or *you.*

MRS CORNWALLIS *cowers as* RITA *forces her around the room.*

A good common sense talk like good common sense people, that's what we need Mrs O-nions.

RITA: I'm not a common sense person thank Christ! I'd sooner be a raving lunatic than have common sense.

AUDREY LEMON *enters, she is wearing some symbol of independence.*

AUDREY: Oh hello! What are you doing now? Is it charades?

LOVETT: It's judo I think. *One* of them.

CONELLY: It's Kung Fu. They're fighting.

She (*She points to* MRS CORNWALLIS.) Wants Rita to go for a cup of tea. And Rita doesn't want one.

AUDREY (*doutbfully*): Oh I see, can I interrupt a weeny mo? Does anyone know where my husband is? He's got all the keys, I can't get into the house, silly aren't I?

LOVETT: Rita made him cry. He's in her office drinking tea. We'll all be in there soon at this rate.

CONELLY: Shall I fetch him? I enjoy walking without me corsets.

AUDREY: Would you mind? I'd rather see him with Rita here, he's got a violent tongue.

RITA: Nobody was ever *licked* to death, Audrey, shout back. You've done it once.

MRS CORNWALLIS: Would you fetch some porters, Mrs Connelly, and ask somebody to telephone the police. Reason has failed, it's time for the civil authorities.

Will you do that for me, dear?

CONELLY: No, I don't feel like it!

CONELLY *goes out.*

MRS CORNWALLIS: This is too much, when even old age pensioners won't do as they're told! It's anarchy, anarchy, and who will attend to the drains? Ask yourselves that, I can feel a small breakdown coming on, do you mind if I sit down?

She sits.

DOLLY: Do you want a drink? You look awful.

RITA: Go on, humanise yourself.

The ASSISTANT HOSPITAL ADMINISTRATOR *drinks from the gin bottle.*

MRS CORNWALLIS: This is the climax of a disastrous day. I was five crates short of prunes in kitchen supplies this morning. Then I discovered that the date stamps on the disposable enema packs ran out yesterday, and being the *Assistant* Administrator I get all the blame.

He's always in a meeting. (*Bitterly:*) Now the patients are talking back, it's never happened before.

AUDREY: Are you going to cry? I've got some tissues if you are.

MRS CORNWALLIS: If you've got them handy I may as well.

MRS CORNWALLIS *cries quietly.*

RITA: You can't help feeling sorry for her, can you? It's like seeing a hot-air balloon being let down.

DOLLY: Aah! Be fair, Rita, she has got a hard job.

RITA: Yes, where would the hospital be without it's prunes and enemas?

LOVETT: Bunged up for a start.

Everyone laughs except MRS CORNWALLIS.

CONELLY (*self-importantly enters*): He says he won't come in if Rita's here.

He says she's mad.

RITA: Where is he?

CONELLY: Outside the door, he's listening.

RITA (*shouting to* JAMES): Get in here! There's somebody needs spiritual guidance!

JAMES: Is it Audrey?

RITA *pulls* JAMES *in, shuts the door and leans on it.*

RITA: No it's me. I want you to tell me something.

There is a pause. She walks about.

Where do I go to catch the ark?

JAMES: You don't catch it, it isn't a bus.

LOVETT: It's a boat!

RITA: I know that. Will it sail up the canal? And how will all you people get in it?

JAMES: The Lord Jehovah will make provision for all his saved souls. Audrey won't be amongst them of course.

AUDREY: I don't *like* boats, I get seasick.

RITA: How big will this ark be?

JAMES: Big.

LOVETT: How will it get down the canals and through all them locks?

JAMES: It will sail over the inland waterways. It will sail over your sinful bodies and we, the saved, will lean over the side and watch the sinners and unbelievers gasping their last breaths in the foaming waters.

CONELLY: He's got a lovely turn of phrase hasn't he?

LOVETT: Will it go to London?

JAMES: It will save all who repent and put their souls in the hands of Jehovah, God.

LOVETT: Yes, but will it go to London?

JAMES: Yes, I expect so, once it's toured the provinces.

LOVETT: Only I've got a cousin in London that's a Jehovah's Witness, she'll be disappointed if you forgot her. She's a miserable sod like you.

CONELLY (*to* JAMES): Audrey wants the keys.

AUDREY: Yes James, could I have the keys?

JAMES: No, I'm the householder, they are *my* keys.

AUDREY: My clothes are in the house, give me the keys.

JAMES: I brought your clothes with my money, they're *my* clothes.

AUDREY: You'd look silly in my clothes, James. They'd be too small. Now give me the keys.

JAMES: No!

AUDREY: Give me the sodding keys!

JAMES: Don't swear, Audrey, think of your mother!

AUDREY *makes a deep throaty noise of anger and lunges at* JAMES's *trouser pocket. She pulls him to the floor, they wrestle over the keys.*

MRS CORNWALLIS: Oh my God! Now there's a fight! I can't cope on my own. I need a man. Where's Mr Riley?

LOVETT: I haven't seen him all afternoon.

RITA: I haven't seen anyone with medical qualifications since I stepped foot in the place.

MRS CORNWALLIS: The hospital is on accident alert, there's a disturbance at the Job Centre.

RITA: Knock on his door, Evelyn, see if he's still in there.

CONELLY: Oh I daren't.

RITA: He's only a man.

CONELLY: No he's not, he's a doctor.

LOVETT: I'll go.

She knocks on RILEY's *door. There is no answer. She knocks again and puts her head round the door.*

He's asleep! Shush!

MRS CORNWALLIS: He can't be asleep, doctors don't sleep!

LOVETT: He must be dead then.

DOLLY: Dead, Oh my God, the doctor's dead!

MRS CORNWALLIS: Mr Riley's manners are impeccable. He wouldn't die in a National Health hospital.

LOVETT: He's not moving.

MRS CORNWALLIS: They'll blame me! It's all the clerk's fault. She should have stayed at her post, instead of coming whining to me. Her job is to protect the doctor from his patients, now they've killed him! I'll get the blame, I always do.

MRS CORNWALLIS *cries loudly. The telephone rings on the* CLERK's *desk. Everyone stops for three seconds, then carries on. The* ASSISTANT HOSPITAL ADMINISTRATOR *answers it.*

(*Giving phone to* RITA): It's for you. You'll be thinking you own the hospital next.

RITA: I do! Me and sixty million others. (*She speaks into the phone:*) Hello!

Pause.

Hang on a minute.

(*She speaks to the* GROUP *who are making a terrible row:*) Shut the bleedin' row, I'm on the phone.

The GROUP *is silent.*

(*She speaks into the phone:*) Already? Hang on.

(*She speaks to the* GROUP:) Lynda's had her baby. It's a girl!

The GROUP *cheer.*

LOVETT, CONELLY, AUDREY, DOLLY: Oh! How lovely! How much does it weight? (*Etc.*)

RITA (*into phone*): My middle name? Mary . . . Oh that's nice, tell her I'll be up to see her when she's had a sleep. (*She puts the phone down and speaks to the* GROUP:) She's calling her baby Mary, that's my middle name.

LOVETT: Isn't that nice. It's quite an honour as how they're posh and that.

CONELLY: Quick with it, wasn't she? It must have been all that yogurt.

AUDREY *and* JAMES's *fighting has turned to passionate embraces.*

AUDREY: James!

JAMES: Audrey!

They make their way into a cubicle.

DOLLY: She'll be a Libra.

LOVETT: Who will?

DOLLY: The baby — Mary. That's a nice sign that is. I wonder what her stars say. I'm a Libra. We're home-lovers and we . . .

RITA: I'm Aries.

DOLLY: They're bossy and can't settle to nothing.

RITA: It's a load of rubbish.

DOLLY: It's not, Rita, it's been proved.

LOVETT: I think it's rubbish. The day my husband was laid-off his stars said 'Job prospects look good'.

CONELLY: I like reading my stars. Once it said 'Your finances will improve' and I found ten pence in the street.

DOLLY: There you are you see.

CONELLY: But I lost a pound the day after.

DOLLY: I bet you're a Leo aren't you, Evelyn?

RITA: Shut up, Dolly, you're always wrong.

DOLLY: I think I'm right this time.

CONELLY: No I'm Capricorn.

DOLLY: Oh well . . . Let's see what your

stars say for the week. Here it is: 'You are embarking on a most exciting period. The future has never looked better.'

CONELLY: It looks like I'm going to have more fun dead than alive.

MRS CORNWALLIS: How can you joke about such a painful subject? There are people in the process of dying upstairs. I find your merriment strangely inappropriate.

CONELLY: Well, I'm in the process of dying down here. (*She laughs.*) If you can prove to me that laughing is harmful, then I'll stop. But until then I'll laugh as much as I like!

RITA: Let's have a toast to Mary . . . I hope she has a bleedin' good laugh all her life.

DOLLY: I wish that she's good-looking and that she ends up with a nice bloke.

LOVETT: To Mary, I hope that she's clever, got brains y' know.

CONELLY: I wish her good health and a long life.

RITA (*to* MRS CORNWALLIS): It's your turn.

MRS CORNWALLIS: I wish the child well certainly.

To the refrain of Stevie Wonder's 'Happy Birthday To You' RILEY *enters.*

RILEY *comes in yawning. He looks at his watch then stands and stares at the scene in front of him.* MRS CORNWALLIS *is holding the gin bottle.* DOLLY *is reading* Woman *with her feet on the* CLERK's *desk.*

Everyone else is watching AUDREY *and* JAMES's *feet in the curtained cubicle.* MRS LOVETT *is laughing,* AUDREY *and* JAMES *are oblivious to everything.* RITA *is handing out the patients' confidential files.*

RITA: Here, read your own file.

DOLLY (*seeing* RILEY): Hello, we thought you were dead!

RILEY: I wish I was.

RITA: Do you feel better for that sleep?

RILEY *crosses to the cubicle and looks over the top, indicating* JAMES *and* AUDREY.

RILEY: Is that Mrs Lemon in the

LOVETT: Yes, with Mr Lemon.

RITA: Well, they started fighting over a bunch of keys. Here, Mrs Conelly.

RITA *passes* CONELLY *her file.*

CONELLY: Thanks, Rita.

MRS CORNWALLIS: Oh! Mr Riley, you're alive!

RILEY: Only just, Mrs Cornwallis, only just.
Is it wise to be seen carrying a bottle of gin around the hospital Mrs Cornwallis?

RITA: Why don't you go and water your rubber plants? I'll get you out of trouble, I don't bear grudges.
Here you are Mrs Lovett.

She gives LOVETT *her file.*

LOVETT: Thanks, I've been dying to get me hands on this.

She reads the file avidly.

MRS CORNWALLIS: Doctor, the patients are rebelling, they won't keep still or quiet.

RILEY: They do seem unusually animated. I'm used to seeing them in rows like dead sheep. Go and tidy up, Mrs Cornwallis. Your eyelashes are falling off.

CONELLY: Hello, Mr Riley, are you all right now?

RILEY: Hello, my dear, still here then?

CONELLY: Yes, I've had a lovely afternoon.

RILEY: Are you coming to see me?

LOVETT: Ooh 'ya bugger, I think he fancies you, Evelyn.

CONELLY: I think he's got a bet on how long I've got left. The Irish *are* betting men.

RITA: Can we start the clinic now, doctor?

RILEY: There should be a list. Where's the clerk?

DOLLY: Oh *she* ran off ages ago.

RITA *sorts out her file.*

RITA: Well if nobody minds, I'll go first. Then we'll all go up and see Lynda's baby later on.

DOLLY: It's not visiting time, Rita, and they only let close family see the baby. They're ever so strict in maternity.

RITA: According to her file, Dr Riley's Lynda's consultant. So we'll all go up with him, won't we Dr Riley?

RILEY: Will you?

RITA: You've got alcohol on your breath Dr Riley.

RILEY: Just a taint dear, just a taint.

RITA *guides* RILEY *into his room.*

RITA: You warm your hands on the radiator, Declan, I won't be long.
(*She speaks to the* GROUP:) Don't let her mess you about. (*She indicates* MRS CORNWALLIS.)
Dolly, take a collection, we'll buy Lynda some flowers.

Pause.

Wish me luck.

RITA *lights a cigarette.*

DOLLY: I'm sure it's not serious, Reet. You'll be all right.

GROUP: Good luck. See you soon.

RITA *goes into the consulting room.*

DOLLY: Well er . . . Does anybody want to start the collection?

LOVETT: I'd like to but I've only got my

bus fare home. We're a bit short right now.

DOLLY: *You* don't work then?

LOVETT: I *was* a school dinner lady.

DOLLY: Oh . . . that's a shame.

CONELLY: I'll put twenty pence in it for you. I got my pension today.

LOVETT: No. I'd sooner walk home than take money from a pensioner.

CONELLY: No, let me! I can afford it. I don't need money any more do I? My insurance is all paid up. (*She laughs.*) It's nice to help somebody for a change.

LOVETT: All right then, but I'll give it back, give me your address before you go.

DOLLY (*to* MRS CORNWALLIS): Will you put some money in?

MRS CORNWALLIS: I hardly think it's apposite. If I sent flowers to every patient in this hospital I'd be a pauper.

LOVETT: You've drunk more than twenty p's worth of gin, so you can give Dolly twenty pence and then Dolly can put it in.

There is an ecstatic groan.

DOLLY: What are they doing in there? (*She indicates the cubicle.*)

LOVETT: Each other by the sound of it.

DOLLY (*clearing her throat and approaching the cubicle*): Excuse me. Excuse me.

LOVETT: Throw a bucket of water over them!

JAMES *and* AUDREY *fall out of the cubicle.*

DOLLY: I'm collecting some money for some flowers for Lynda, would you like to . . .

MRS CORNWALLIS: Mr Lemon, I have no wish to see your underwear. Please adjust the opening of your trousers.

LOVETT: I bet this is the first time she's seen a bloke's underwear . . . with a bloke in it.

MRS CORNWALLIS: I heard that. I fail to see the humour in a man disporting himself in public. Quite frankly I'm disgusted with you, Mr Lemon. I think you must have some perverse sense of social decorum.

LOVETT: That's the second time you've been called a pervert.

AUDREY: James is a perfectly normal man. And if anyone says one more word about him being a pervert, I shall have to scratch their eyes out.

JAMES: Audrey darling!

They embrace.

MRS CORNWALLIS: That's enough, Mr Lemon. Pull yourself together and move these benches back. We require a man's strength.

JAMES, *with a passionate look at his wife, does as he is told.*

What has happened this afternoon will never happen again. Is that clear? So we're going to start by sitting down and keeping quiet. And you can give me those files back. They are private and confidential.

LOVETT: I've read mine.

MRS CORNWALLIS: Quiet!

There is a long pause as everyone settles back to normal.

DOLLY: I've remembered that word.

LOVETT: What, Rita's word?

DOLLY: Yes. It's activist, she's an activist.

LOVETT: Never heard of it.

Blackout.

Methuen Modern Plays

include work by

Jean Anouilh
John Arden
Margaretta D'Arcy
Brendan Behan
Edward Bond
Bertolt Brecht
Howard Brenton
Mikhail Bulgakov
Noel Coward
Shelagh Delaney
David Edgar
Michael Frayn
Max Frisch
Jean Giraudoux
Simon Gray
Peter Handke
Vaclav Havel
Kaufman & Hart
Barrie Keeffe
Arthur Kopit
John McGrath
David Mercer
Arthur Miller
Mtwa, Ngema & Simon
Peter Nichols
Joe Orton
Harold Pinter
Luigi Pirandello
Stephen Poliakoff
David Rudkin
Jean-Paul Sartre
Wole Soyinka
C.P. Taylor
Peter Whelan
Nigel Williams

Methuen Young Drama

The Business of Good Government	a nativity play by John Arden and Margaretta D'Arcy, with production notes on costumes, properties and the singing of the music
Sweetie Pie	a play about women in society devised by Bolton Octagon Theatre-in-Education Company, edited and introduced by Eileen Murphy for 14 year-olds upwards
Old King Cole	a play by Ken Campbell originally written for the Victoria Theatre, Stoke-on-Trent for 8-12 year-olds
Skungpoomery	a play by Ken Campbell originally written for the Nottingham Playhouse Roundabout Company for 7-13 year-olds
Timesneeze	a participatory play by David Campton originally written for the Young Vic for 7-11 year-olds
The Incredible Vanishing!	a play by Denise Coffey originally written for the Young Vic for 8-12 year-olds
The Adventures of Awful Knawful	a play by Peter Flannery and Mick Ford originally written for the RSC Kids' Show for 7-11 year-olds
One Cool Cat	a play by John Laing, winner of the 1983 Play for Polka Competition for 6-10 year-olds
Pongo Plays 1-6	six short plays by Henry Livings with music by Alex Glasgow for 12 year-olds upwards
Six More Pongo Plays	six short plays by Henry Livings with music by Alex Glasgow for 12 year-olds upwards
Our Day Out	a musical play by Willy Russell with

	songs by Willy Russell, Bob Eaton and Chris Mellors
Theatre-in-Education programmes	INFANTS edited by Pam Schweitzer five programmes for 5-8 year-olds JUNIORS edited by Pam Schweitzer four programmes for 8-12 year-olds SECONDARY edited by Pam Schweitzer four programmes for 12 year-olds upwards
School For Clowns	a play by F.K. Waechter translated by Ken Campbell for 7-14 year-olds
Live Theatre	Four Plays for Young People by C.P. Taylor originally staged by the Tyneside touring Live Theatre Co.
Theatre Box	five plays for 8-12 year-olds from the Thames Television Theatre Box series. They have been adapted by Jonathan Dudley so that they can be staged by or for children and with the minimum of apparatus or as lavishly as funds permit.

MARMALADE ATKINS
by Andrew Davies
DEATH ANGEL
by Brian Glover
REASONS TO BE CHEERFUL
by James Andrew Hall
YOU MUST BELIEVE ALL THIS
by Adrian Mitchell
THE PRINCE AND THE DEMONS
by George Moore

If you would like to receive, free of charge, regular information about new plays and theatre books from Methuen, please send your name and address to:

The Marketing Department (Drama)
Methuen London Ltd
North Way
Andover
Hampshire SP10 5BE